THE POWER OF
EVERYDAY
MISSIONARIES

THE POWER OF
EVERYDAY
MISSIONARIES

THE WHAT AND HOW
OF SHARING THE GOSPEL

CLAYTON M. CHRISTENSEN

DESERET
BOOK

Salt Lake City, Utah

Proceeds from the sale of this book will be donated to the general missionary fund of
The Church of Jesus Christ of Latter-day Saints.

Library of Congress Cataloging-in-Publication Data

Christensen, Clayton M., author.
  The power of everyday missionaries : the what and how of sharing the gospel / Clayton M.
Christensen.
      pages cm
  Includes bibliographical references.
  ISBN 978-1-60907-315-2 (paperbound)
  ISBN 978-1-60907-316-9 (hardbound)
  1. Evangelistic work—The Church of Jesus Christ of Latter-day Saints. 2. Mormon missionaries.
3. The Church of Jesus Christ of Latter-day Saints—Missions. I. Title.
  BX8661.C43 2013
  266'.9332—dc23   2012043321

Printed in the United States of America
Publishers Printing, Salt Lake City, UT

10

Contents

We invite you to visit frequently our website
everydaymissionaries.org
as you read this book. Tell other readers what you learn as
you follow the principles for sharing the gospel—and
tell your stories that will inspire the rest of us!

The Blessings That Come from Sharing the Gospel

My purpose in writing this book is simply to offer my witness that being a member missionary can be a source of deep happiness. It need not be hard. You will pull wonderful friends into your life because they will be able to feel your love for them when you invite them to learn more about their Heavenly Father. And every time you take someone figuratively by the hand and introduce him or her to Jesus Christ, you will feel how deeply our Savior loves you and loves the person whose hand is in yours.

I have spent a very large portion of my life working to build the kingdom of God through missionary work—and in so doing have worked hard to understand what God told Isaiah: "For my thoughts are not your thoughts, neither are your ways my ways" (Isaiah 55:8). Among other things, I have learned that Satan's work to slow our missionary efforts is not just manifest in tempting us as individuals to break God's commandments. He also tries to guide us to depend upon the thoughts and ways of man as we share the gospel.

Many of us know people who seem to be "natural missionaries," almost as if they have an innate gift that makes sharing the gospel easy for them. My wife, Christine, and I certainly are *not* naturals at this. We found the work to be uncomfortable and intimidating at the outset, which I recognize in retrospect was because we were following many of the thoughts and ways of man. Learning and following the principles summarized in this book have helped us share the gospel in ways that have become natural and energizing because, I believe, we are following more completely God's ways in doing missionary work.*

In a vision of our time, Daniel saw that "in the days of these kings shall the God of heaven set up a kingdom, which shall never be destroyed: and the kingdom shall not be left to other people, but it shall break in pieces and consume all these kingdoms, and it shall stand for ever" (Daniel 2:44).

There are currently more than 14 million members in the restored Church of Jesus Christ—so we must be doing something right. There is cause for concern, however. The Church is indeed growing rapidly in some parts of Africa, Latin America, and Southeast Asia, in what economists call the developing world. But many of us in prosperous nations have concluded that the kingdom in our homelands is done growing. In a stake near Boston, for example, nearly seventy-five members of two adjacent wards moved out of the area in a time of economic downturn. The two wards were subsequently merged to continue the feeling among the remaining members that the ward was "strong." Somehow, the leaders and members didn't seem to seriously consider a second

---

*In this book I'll typically use the word *we* rather than *I* when I refer to things that I and my wife, Christine; my children, Matthew, Ann, Michael, Spencer, and Katie; and my friends and colleagues have collectively learned about sharing the gospel. I will speak in the first person whenever I recount an experience that was my own.

option, which would have been to find seventy-five new members who might accept the gospel from among the 100,000 not-yet-members who lived in the areas of these wards.

Was Daniel's vision little more than wishful thinking? I don't think so. Indeed, the Lord's statement that the world is "white already to harvest" (D&C 4:4) doesn't have an expiration date. The world is still ready.

I have observed that when we do not magnify our callings, much of the time it is because we don't know *how* to do so. Most of us are *very* anxious to be great member missionaries. The problem is that we just don't know how to follow God's thoughts and his ways. I hope that this book will help those of us who want to wield our sickles with our might to become great member missionaries.*

Feeling the Spirit of God Again

Let me describe how sharing the gospel has been such a source of happiness for me. After I finished business school at age twenty-seven and began my career, in imperceptible increments I began to feel the Spirit less and less in my life. I was serving as a counselor to Bishop Kent Bowen in Boston, and I was spending a lot of time and energy to magnify that assignment. I was praying and studying the scriptures regularly, and yet despite my doing all these "right" things, I just felt that the Spirit was not with me as much as I had felt it when I was on my mission in Korea.

Then we moved to Washington, D.C., where I was to work as

---

*Preach My Gospel is a marvelous tool that helps full-time missionaries learn how to do their work. While its teachings are useful for everyone, its focus is not to teach the rest of us *how* to share the gospel—how to find people who are excited to meet with the missionaries and how to support the missionaries to guide them toward baptism.

a White House Fellow. All of a sudden, we lived and worked and commuted with new people, and I found myself with many more opportunities to discuss the gospel with my new friends. In short order after our move, two of my colleagues accepted my invitation to come to our home and take the missionary discussions.

Before one of our lessons with them, we were scurrying around to clean things up. I put a tape of the Mormon Youth Symphony and Chorus into our stereo, and the choir began playing their rendition of "The Spirit of God" (*Hymns,* no. 2). I was in the dining room when they began the third verse:

> *We'll call in our solemn assemblies in spirit,*
> *To spread forth the kingdom of heaven abroad,*
> *That we through our faith may begin to inherit*
> *The visions and blessings and glories of God.*

As I heard those words, a powerful and sweet spirit entered my heart, and I realized what had been happening in my spiritual life. With our move to Washington, I had begun again to do my part in spreading forth the kingdom of heaven abroad. And what I inherited as a result were the visions and blessings and glories of God. I had begun feeling the Spirit again on a daily basis. My dreams were about spiritual things, and I was singing the hymns of the Restoration as I walked to the bus stop.

I'll summarize the lesson I learned from this with a metaphor. In a war, the generals give the state-of-the-art weapons to those soldiers who are on the front lines engaged in direct combat with the enemy. To those of their troops who work in administrative positions behind the lines, they'll give less-potent tools. What had happened in Boston was that I had been spending more of my Church service on administrative things. I actually could do most of those kinds of things effectively, without needing to rely very heavily on the Spirit. But in becoming an active missionary again, I had essentially repositioned myself onto the front lines in the war against Satan over the souls of men. This meant that I needed the Spirit with me every day.

Hence, under license given to each of us in section 4 of the Doctrine and Covenants, I "called myself" on a mission. I love my life as a missionary, keeping myself on the front lines. The image in my mind is that God, my General, stands at the door when I go out every morning; and, knowing what the war is like, day after day He gives me His most powerful weapon: His Spirit. For this I am grateful.

Impact on Our Family

The blessings that have come to our family from being missionaries have been incalculable. Several years ago, for example, we invited one of my former students, Sunil, to take the missionary discussions in our home. The missionaries did a wonderful job, and at the close of the first lesson they both testified of the truths they had taught us. Christine and I bore our testimonies as well, and I then asked one of the missionaries to close with prayer. Just then our son Spencer, who had been sitting quietly on the piano bench, raised his hand and asked, "Dad, can I say something?" He then rose to his feet and, looking at Sunil with a pure gaze, said, "Sunil, I'm only eleven years old. But I want you to know that the things the missionaries have told you tonight are true. I know that God lives. I know that you and I are His sons and that Joseph Smith was truly a prophet of God." As he shared his feelings, a sweet, powerful spirit came into the room.

The next day Sunil sent an email saying that although he had appreciated the clear explanation of our beliefs that the missionaries had provided during the discussion, "when your young son stood and said those words, I felt something inside that I have never felt before. This must be what you mean when you speak of the Spirit of God."

Many blessings and friendships have come into our lives from our trying to share the gospel. But this blessing has been one of the best: Having the missionaries regularly help us as a family teach the gospel to new and old friends through the power of the Holy Ghost has profoundly affected the faith of our five children and brought the Spirit of God into our home.

Promised Blessings to Every Member

Would the kingdom of God spin out of balance if all of its members similarly called themselves as missionaries? Much of the Church is organized into programs, everything from home and visiting teaching to auxiliary organizations to family history, welfare, and public affairs. When called to serve in the Church, we often frame our responsibilities in terms of these programs and the subset of members who are served by them. When asked to describe her assignment, for example, a Primary president might say that she is responsible for the children in her ward aged eighteen months to twelve years—that every Sunday morning she organizes sharing time, supervises nursery workers, and oversees teachers who instruct each age group of children. Scoutmasters shoulder responsibility for the Scouting program for boys aged twelve and thirteen. And so on.

These programs help us implement the purposes of the Church, which include preaching the gospel, perfecting the Saints, redeeming the dead, and administering relief to the needy. Framing our responsibilities by program imparts tidiness to the Church. It tells us what we are responsible for and what we are *not* responsible for. This programmatic framing also imparts a sense of trade-offs, however. We become concerned that overemphasizing one program necessarily starves another of the time, oversight, energy, and talent that it warrants. To the busy, trade-offs seem immutable.

Prompted by the Lord's reminder, "For my thoughts are not your thoughts, neither are your ways my ways" (Isaiah 55:8), several friends—Elder Bob Gay, Elder Matt Eyring, David Wingate—and I decided to search the Doctrine and Covenants to see what guidance it might offer our ward and stake leaders for balancing these trade-offs to achieve proper focus. We found that the Doctrine and Covenants, as the instruction that God gave us for building the kingdom of God in the latter days, is filled with remarkable promises that God has offered to those who accept His call to share the gospel. Far from putting the kingdom out of balance, if our ward and stake leaders were to focus on leading their members to share the gospel, many of the other problems that fester in our hearts and homes, and in our wards and stakes, would resolve themselves through the blessings that come from accepting the call that God has given each of us to be missionaries.

Some promises relate to the power and strength people will receive as they share the gospel (the section and verse of the Doctrine and Covenants in which these promises are given are shown in parentheses):

- None shall stay you (1:5).
- You shall receive strength such as is not known among men (24:12).
- He Himself will go with you and be in your midst. Nothing shall prevail against you (32:3).

- Power shall rest upon you. He will be with you and go before your face (39:12).
- Your enemies will not have power over you (44:5).
- The Lord will stand by you (68:6).
- No weapon formed against you shall prosper (71:9).
- He will uphold you (93:51).
- The gates of hell shall not prevail against you (17:8).
- You shall have power to declare His word (99:2).
- Your tongue shall be loosed, and you will have the power of God unto the convincing of men (11:21).
- Your mouth shall be filled and you shall become even as Nephi of old (33:8).
- You will not be confounded. It shall be given you in the very hour that portion that shall be meted unto every man (84:85; 100:5).
- Your words shall be scripture, shall be the will of the Lord, shall be the mind of the Lord, and shall be the voice of the Lord and the power of God unto salvation (68:4).
- Your arm will be God's arm. He will be your shield and buckler; He will gird up your loins and put your enemies under your feet (35:14).

Other blessings the Lord has promised to those who share the gospel relate to personal purity and increased faith:

- You shall stand blameless before God (4:2).
- You shall be lifted up at the last day (17:8).
- You will be given a testimony of the words of the prophets (21:9).
- You shall have revelations (28:8).

- Your sins will be forgiven (31:5; 36:1; 60:7; 62:3; 84:61).
- You shall have great faith (39:12).
- You will be able to keep God's laws (44:5).

Consider the blessings that pertain to happiness, health, and prosperity:

- You shall have blessings greater than the treasures of earth (19:37–38).
- He will take care of your flocks (88:72), and your back shall be laden with sheaves (31:5; 33:9).
- You shall not be weary in mind, body, limb, or joint, and you shall not go hungry or thirsty. A hair from your head shall not fall to the ground unnoticed (84:80, 116).
- Your joy shall be great (18:14–15).

And perhaps most extraordinary of all, He has promised to fill us and our work with the Holy Ghost, to make us into better men and women:

- He will send upon you the Comforter, which shall teach you the truth and the way whither you shall go (79:2).
- The Holy Ghost shall be shed forth in bearing record of all things, whatsoever ye shall say (100:8).
- He will go before your face. He will be on your right hand and on your left; His Spirit shall be in your hearts, and His angels round about you, to bear you up. (84:88).
- He will bear you up as on eagles' wings; and you shall beget glory and honor to yourself and unto the Lord's name (124:18).
- He will make you holy (60:7).

We share the gospel because we know it will help others become better, happier people. But the blessings for us are priceless. What bishop wouldn't want these promises to be fulfilled in his life and the lives of each member of his ward? What parents wouldn't want them for their children? What individuals wouldn't want these blessings for themselves?

Sharing the gospel doesn't just *require* that we have the power of God unto the convincing of men. It *gives* us this power. It will magnify our words to be scripture: to be the will of the Lord, the mind of the Lord, the voice of the Lord, and the power of God unto salvation.

Missionary work will help those of us who are battling against addictions and bad habits and are struggling to feel worthy, to stand blameless before God, to become forgiven of our sins, and to have the strength to keep God's laws. It doesn't just demand our purity. It will *help* us be pure. For those of us who struggle with sadness, sharing the gospel will give us great joy. It will make us become holy men and women who have great revelations and are borne up from our burdens as on eagles' wings, begetting glory and honor to ourselves and unto the Lord's name. Involving our children in sharing the gospel is a plan to develop in each of them a testimony of the words of the prophets and to help them become young men and women of great faith.

We all accepted God's call to serve as member missionaries—as witnesses of Him—when we were baptized (see Mosiah 18:10). As promised, the Lord will fill our lives with the blessings listed previously if we will begin sharing the gospel, rekindling the Spirit we felt when we were full-time missionaries or when we accepted the gospel ourselves. And whatever our other responsibilities in the kingdom of God might be, we will become more successful in those callings and in our personal efforts to become pure disciples of Christ when sharing the gospel becomes part of all that we do. Of this I bear witness.

But Where Do I Start?

A premise of this book is that in callings that we are given to build some portion of the kingdom of God, we must know *what* we need to do and we must know *how* to do it. Often the "what" of a calling is conveyed reasonably clearly. But teaching us how to do it is sometimes neglected.

To see why this is so important, consider the calling of a Primary president in the typical ward. Most ward Primary presidents succeed in this calling. Why? I believe it is because the women in this assignment have been taught both *what* they need to do and *how* to do it. The "what" typically is conveyed in scriptures, handbooks, and conference talks. The "how to do it" is taught in two ways: by role models—others who have previously served in that calling—and by a structure that defines everyone's roles and schedules. The structure in Primary includes sharing time, singing time, manuals for each age group, and a schedule that delineates when each of these needs to be done. The role models are previous incumbents who masterfully magnified that calling. Structure and role modeling are important reasons why most of the Primary presidents that I have known have been successful. They know what to do and how to do it.

In contrast, there are other callings in the Church in which members frequently flounder. They have a vague sense for what they are supposed to do but no idea how to do it. There is little structure to their work, and few visible and successful role models are available to emulate. Ward employment specialists and provident living specialists are examples of such callings. It is really hard for most members to feel successful when they serve in these assignments. Likewise, the leverage for accelerating the building of the kingdom of God is not to somehow find "better" or "more converted" members. Rather, it is to teach us *how* to do it.

The Savior, as leader and teacher, was a master at the "what" and the "how." He has told us what to do, by giving us commandments. And He told us how to do it, by giving us stories and parables. The brother of Jared, the good Samaritan, and the prodigal son are role models for how He taught. Their actions don't dictate the specifics, but they illustrate principles that we can draw upon when we know what we must do but don't know how to do it.

Perhaps one reason missionary work is slowing down in so many portions of the earth is that we as members don't know how to share the gospel. It is a pervasive problem in this work. Most of us don't know how to find people for the missionaries to teach. Most of those whom the missionaries begin teaching either stop investigating the gospel short of baptism or fall away shortly afterward. There are some factors we might consider in asking why this happens: often we never teach our friends who are investigating the gospel how to truly pray, how to read the scriptures meaningfully, how to ponder and listen to God. Many investigators stop short— not because they don't want to get a testimony but because they just don't know how to get it.

Although they do magnificently in most dimensions of their callings, many bishops flounder with the responsibility for missionary work in their wards. They know what they are supposed to do, but they just don't know how to lead the effort. Bishops and ward mission leaders should work hand in glove, but ward mission leaders are often adrift, serving more as administrators than as *leaders*—because they don't know how to lead the members.

These are the reasons why I have written this book. I hope

that by the end you will have concluded that the ability to share the gospel isn't a "gift" that has been given to only a few Latter-day Saints and denied to the rest. Finding people for the missionaries to teach and helping them progress toward baptism can be easy and natural for *all* of us if we learn how to do this in ways that mirror the mind and the ways of God. I invite you to view the stories in this book as parables from which you can glean principles that are applicable to your situation.

The book is structured in three sections. Part 1 attempts to show how we can find people to introduce to the missionaries to teach. Part 2 focuses on how to help those who are investigating the Church progress more resolutely toward baptism and a life of committed membership. Part 3 shares some latter-day miracles that show in action some principles that can help missionary work move forward on all fronts. In every chapter I have tried to teach "how" in the way that the Savior taught: through parables. In this case, each of these parables is a true story. These are stories, for the most part, that happened to me or to other members of the Church in New England who have told them to me. I have disguised their names and other personal details as needed to protect their interests. I am not recounting these stories in any way to put us on a hill to be admired. I use them simply to show what we have tried to do, what has worked and what has not, and what we have learned from each other about how to do what God wants us to do. I hope that these will help you, too.

PART 1

FINDING PEOPLE FOR THE MISSIONARIES TO TEACH

Tracting, or door-to-door contacting, is demonstrably the least effective way for full-time missionaries to find people to teach. It takes a great deal of time and effort, and much wading through discouragement and frustration, to find a "golden" contact in this way.

Add to this the fact that the world is changing. With people becoming less willing to open their doors to strangers, the effectiveness of tracting is diminishing rapidly. As time goes by, more and more of the people whom we want the missionaries to be able to teach live in apartment buildings or gated communities into which missionaries cannot enter unescorted. And as more two-career families become the norm, there is often nobody at home when the missionaries knock.

This all means that in the future the members will need to accept a much larger role in finding people for the missionaries to teach. But how is this to be done? This section discusses a number of principles that demonstrate that you might be closer than you think to inviting people to hear about the gospel.

CHAPTER 1

Fundamental Principles: We Cannot Predict and Should Not Judge

Christine and I learned early in our efforts to be good member missionaries that we simply can't predict who will or won't be interested in the gospel. In addition, we have learned that building a friendship is not a prerequisite to inviting people to learn about the gospel. These simple principles have made sharing the gospel much easier.

We discovered these principles when we were newlyweds and the missionaries in our ward asked us to make a list of people with whom we could share the gospel. We were to start with those at the top of our list and begin "preparing" them through a twelve-step process. First, we were to invite them to our home for dinner and follow that by going to a cultural event together. The sixth, seventh, and eighth steps were to invite them to church, give them a copy of the Book of Mormon, and ask them to take the missionary discussions. The program culminated in the twelfth step—baptism.

We dutifully made this list, placing those we thought most likely to be interested in the gospel at the top, and we taped it inside our cupboard. The couple at the top, Ken and Suzy Gray, looked like "ideal Mormons"—people who could have been selected to star in a Church movie by the central casting department in BYU's movie operations. Ken and Suzy's clean living and commitment to family mirrored our own. We began building a friendship with them by inviting them to dinner. They reciprocated with a lovely dinner in their home, and over the next weeks we engaged in a tit-for-tat, finding more and more things to do with the Grays, which began building our friendship with them—exactly as the missionaries suggested would happen. But sharing the gospel began to loom ahead of us as a *big* job, adding additional social events to build new friendships, on top of our already busy lives as Young Men and Young Women leaders in the Oxford Ward.

When we got to step six on the chart, we invited the Grays to church with us, and they accepted—in part because Christine and I had been asked to be the sacrament meeting speakers. It was so exciting. We felt like we were being good member missionaries! After church we had lunch in our home, and I then offered them a copy of the Book of Mormon, asking them if they would be interested in learning more about our church. Ken awkwardly accepted the book and responded, "Thanks, but no thanks. We were both raised in the Episcopalian Church, and we've really enjoyed attending the Church of England while we have been here." We then changed the topic of conversation, but it clearly felt strained, and the Grays left shortly thereafter.

After we washed the dishes, I looked at the chart. "I am *so* disappointed. What should we do?" I asked myself. "I am *so* busy in my studies. And we are *so* busy with the young men and women in the ward." If the Grays weren't interested, our instructions said that we need to develop a friendship with the Baileys (the next people on our list) to prepare them by transforming them into friends (they were simply acquaintances) before we could invite them to learn more. So I found a pencil and crossed the Grays off the list. I felt bad doing this, but we wanted to be good missionaries—and we couldn't work to become friends with everyone.

We invited the Baileys to dinner. They seemed to be pleased to be invited, and so we started the same process we had followed with the Grays. They balked at step six, however, declining our invitation to come to church. So I crossed them off, and we started with the third couple on the list.

At about this time an LDS friend of mine, Randy, who also knew Ken Gray, cornered me at the gym and asked, "Clay, what did you do to make Ken so mad at you?"

I responded that I had no idea. "We did a lot of things with them. They went to church, but they aren't interested in learning more."

Randy explained, "This is Ken's account. All of a sudden you expressed an interest in being friends. But as soon as he told you that he wasn't interested in becoming a Mormon, you dropped the friendship idea like a hot potato. You haven't even talked to him since. You were just wanting to convert them, under the false guise of friendship."

Randy's report hurt, but basically he had gotten the story right. "But what do you want me to do, Randy?" I responded defensively. "God wants us to be missionaries. The mission president says that the best way to do it is first to prepare people to accept your invitation by making them your friends. Then you can invite them. The problem is that if they're not interested, how can I keep cultivating all these friendships, when there is so much else that I need to do?"

I remember thinking, well, we might be making some mistakes, but at least we were trying. One by one, however, those we thought might be interested in learning about the gospel declined our invitations when we got to steps six through eight. In their own way, each of these friends told us they were happy in their present approach to religion. After much work over many months, we didn't find anyone who was interested in learning more about the gospel. We took the chart off the fridge with the conclusion that we just weren't cut out to be member missionaries.

New missionaries were then transferred to our ward. Knowing nothing of our history, they came to our home, unfolded an identical chart on our table, and asked us to make a list of people with whom we could cultivate friendships in preparation for teaching them the gospel. We protested, "We've tried this. It took a long time and didn't work." We explained that we felt we had honestly tried with everyone we thought was a candidate for hearing the discussions.

Desperate for a referral, the missionaries pleaded, "Don't you know *anyone* we could visit?" We gave them the names of four couples we had excluded from our initial list. Among them were the Taylors. We warned that while the elders certainly could knock on the Taylors' door, it would be a waste of time. The husband had bad feelings about organized religion of any kind. In addition, he was a tough rugby player and *loved* his daily pints of Guinness ale.

The elders returned an hour later, jubilant. The Taylors had invited them in, listened to the first discussion, and invited them back for the second. We subsequently became close friends with the Taylors as we studied the missionary discussions together. We would never have imagined that they would have had any interest in the gospel.

We learned from this experience that we simply cannot know in advance who will and will not be interested in learning about the Church. We thought we could judge and therefore excluded from our list many people whose lifestyle, habits, or appearance made them seem unlikely candidates. As we reflect upon those who have joined the Church, however, few of them would have been on our list of "likely members" when they first encountered the Church. "For the Lord seeth not as man seeth; for man looketh on the outward appearance, but the Lord looketh on the heart" (1 Samuel 16:7). Living the gospel transforms them. The only way *all* people can have the opportunity to choose or reject the gospel of Jesus Christ is for us, without judgment, to invite them to follow the Savior.

This experience also taught us that we don't need to transform our relationships into friendships as a prerequisite to inviting others to learn about the gospel. Whether our platform with people is as neighbors, classmates, work associates, store clerks, or those riding on the same bus, there is no requirement to change that platform before we can invite them. Indeed, we need not and *should* not alter our relationships with others in order to invite them.

Full-time missionaries, for example, don't wait to become friends with their contacts. They talk with everyone. A relationship of trust is built when they have the chance to teach. Over the past twenty years, we have observed no correlation between the depth of a relationship and the probability that a person will be interested in learning about the gospel. But the reverse is almost always true: Everyone who accepts an invitation to learn about the gospel becomes a closer friend, regardless of whether or not he or she ultimately accepts baptism. We have also learned that even when people decline our invitations, they are not offended as long as they can feel our honesty, our love, and God's love when we invite them to learn about Christ's gospel. They typically have expressed gratitude that we cared enough about them to want to share something so personal and important.

More often than you'd like, people say to a coworker, "Watch out. He's a Mormon." When you hear that, almost always it was caused by a member of the Church who feigned friendship in the mistaken belief that we had to "prepare" them before we could invite them. This belief creates among many a distrust of members of our Church, as if Mormons always have an ulterior motive. We must be honest, loving, and direct. These are God's ways.

What Is Success?

Despite seeing much truth and goodness in our Church, the Taylors decided after five of the six lessons that they didn't want to be baptized. Even though we know that many who discontinue investigating will later listen and accept the gospel, we were disappointed. But this taught us our third valuable lesson about member missionary work—we realized we had *succeeded* as missionaries. The Taylors had become great friends, and we had given them the opportunity to understand the gospel of Jesus Christ more deeply. Whether or not they ever enter the waters of baptism, they have taken a step along the path of their own eternal progression and have made some important correct choices.

My friend Ben told me this story that occurred as he was trying to be a better missionary. "First, Clay, you say that you can't predict in advance who, of all the people you'll meet, is going to be interested in learning about the gospel—right? Second, as a general rule you say that about one of four people whom you invite will say 'yes.' This means that you'll hear 'no' three times for each 'yes' you'll hear. Right? That is a hard one because I am fragile about things like this. If I fail the first time, it is really hard for me to try again," Ben explained.

Then he continued, "But I figured out how to solve this paradox. I promised the Lord that I would find someone who would say 'no' to my invitation. That's right. Someone who will say 'no.' *That* is easy. Sure enough, the first person I asked said 'no'—and I had succeeded! Finding someone to say 'no' was a lot easier than I had thought!"

Ben then set a goal to find three additional people to say 'no.' The next person surprised Ben by accepting! That was all it took for Ben. He learned that inviting people really is easy because you succeed when you invite, regardless of how it turns out.

Nothing succeeds like success. My faith deepens every time I invite someone. This is a key reason why making a single initial invitation, like Ben did, can be so important: because it helps you feel the seed grow (see Alma 32). As the seed grows, you begin to believe that God can actually help you find someone to hear the missionary discussions, if you will just do your part and invite. This understanding has made missionary work much easier for me.

I learned this principle even more deeply a few years ago when I had a conversation with a friend at work, Wes Lambert. Wes spoke of the influence that the Mormons he had known at the Harvard Business School had had on his life. "Because of you guys, I decided it wasn't right to live with my girlfriend, so we got married. Because I saw how much happiness your children brought you, we decided to have kids—we now have two. When I saw that your families are so important to you that you don't work weekends, I stopped working weekends too. I've even started going to temple on Saturday. But there's still one difference between you Mormons and me. It's clear that you do what you do because you love God. I'm going to church because I fear God."

I replied that he was right: We do what we do because we love God. Later that day via email, I invited him and his wife to our home so that we could explain how we had come to know and love God. I promised Wes that he could know and love Him too.

A couple of days later I saw Wes and asked if he'd be willing to do this. He thanked me very graciously for caring enough to offer, but then turned me down flat. "We're committed to the traditions of our church, and I have hope that I can find what you're offering within our tradition."

I was crushed. But in the midst of that feeling, I was filled with a very strong impression—almost as if an unseen person were standing beside me—that Jesus loved Wes Lambert. His love for Wes was completely unaffected by the fact that Wes had just rejected this opportunity to learn of Him. Jesus loved Wes so deeply that He already had suffered for all of the sins that Wes might commit—in the off chance that Wes might accept Him when invited to do so. This is how I know that we succeed when we invite.

Moroni saw it too:

"And it came to pass that I prayed unto the Lord that he would give unto the Gentiles grace, that they might have charity.

"And it came to pass that the Lord said unto me: If they have not charity it mattereth not unto thee, thou hast been faithful; wherefore, thy garments shall be made clean" (Ether 12:36–37).

Most of us fear failure. Once we have realized that *we succeed as member missionaries when we invite people to learn and accept the truth,* much of the fear that kept us from sharing the gospel vanishes. We give them the opportunity to exercise their free agency. Some will use that agency to accept the gospel. Others will not, and that's fine. We succeed when we invite.

CHAPTER 2

Create Conversations about the Gospel

How can you engage in discussions with others about our church, even as you face the fact that you can't judge who is and who isn't interested in what it has to offer? Three habits have become helpful to us.

USE MORMON WORDS IN EVERY CONVERSATION

A friend gave me the first idea: to use religious words and "Mormon" words in my day-to-day conversations, such as these:

"I am *so* tired. I am the scoutmaster in our troop sponsored by the LDS Church, and I took the boys on an overnight camping trip last night."

"I go to the Mormon Church in Belmont, and a friend who gave the sermon last Sunday said something that is exactly how we need to start this presentation."

"When I was a Mormon missionary in Korea . . ."

"My daughter who is a student at BYU . . ."

And so on.

When I use these words in my conversation, it is like I am opening a door for people to a conversation about the Church. The vast majority, of course, don't walk through the door, and that's fine. But sometimes they walk through the door by asking, "Oh—so you're a Mormon?"

I respond, "I am, and it is a wonderful church. Why do you ask?" I have found it very helpful to ask, "Why do you ask?" rather than telling them information that they do not care about. This way, we can have a conversation about what *they're* interested in. Most of the time their interest is transitory, and that is fine. But on occasion the person will show even more interest, which then gives me the chance to invite them to have a deeper conversation.

It is important to view normal conversations with people in probabilistic terms. If 5 percent of people have some latent interest in the LDS Church, and I open up a conversational door about the church with twenty people, one of them will express interest—and I can't judge who it will be. If we open a door to a hundred people, five of them will be interested. This is why it is so important to make the gospel a part of our conversations in an open, matter-of-fact way.

What We're Interested In Isn't What They Are Interested In

When someone says, "Tell me about the Mormon Church," we often give a doctrinal response—eternal families, modern prophets and scriptures, and so on. This makes sense to *us* because doctrine is the reason why we are in our church instead of in another. Doctrine over time becomes very important to converts, too. But it typically is not the initial reason for their interest.

In 1975, the Church did an extensive survey of new converts

to determine what it was about the Church that had initially inter-ested them (see L.F. Anderson, "What Are Nonmembers Interested In?" *Ensign,* October 1977). These were the results, in order of frequency of mention:

1. The feeling of closeness to God that they wanted to experi-ence because they could see this closeness in the lives of Mormons they knew.

2. Happiness and a sense of peace, which they wanted and which they saw in the lives of Mormons they knew.

3. They wanted a better sense of purposefulness and direction in their lives. They tended to see this in Mormons they knew.

Only 9 percent of new converts said that doctrine was the main thing that attracted them to the Church. For all who are bap-tized and remain active, doctrine becomes much of the glue that cements them in the Church. But it typically isn't what they were looking for at the outset.

What this means is that when someone gives us a chance to tell them about us, as a general rule we ought not to tell them what *we* like about our own church—about the doctrine that we love so much. Rather, when I respond with a question like "It's a great church. Why do you ask?" if they don't have anything specific in mind, I then answer with something relating to the three reasons noted above. If they have something more specific in mind, then I can answer specifically.

DECOUPLING

The third habit is one that I use with people I know well. I decouple my invitation to learn about the Church from my re-lationship with them, using language like this: "Scott, I'm going to ask you a question. But before I ask, we need to agree that our friendship won't be affected if you decide that this isn't of interest to you. Okay?" Almost always, they assure me that this is all right. Then I say, "As you know, I'm a member of the LDS Church. For a while I've just had a sense that there are a few aspects about the Church that might be interesting to you. If at some point you have an interest, I'd love the chance to talk a bit about these things."

By couching my invitation in this way, I make it easy for them to say no, and as a consequence it doesn't strain my relationship with them at all. In fact, whether or not they have an interest, almost always they will thank me for caring enough about them to ask.

DISCOVERING THEIR QUESTIONS

Many churches of mainstream Protestant and Catholic religions are largely empty. I learned something about this supposed disinterest in religion that is flooding the developed world through an experience I had with a man that I met several years ago named Stephen Spencer. Asking sincere questions about someone's supposed disinterest in religion is another way to engage in conversations about the gospel.

In our first conversation, I used Mormon words, and he verified, "Oh, so you're a Mormon?"

I replied, "Yeah, that's me. Why do you ask? It really is a great church, by the way."

He said, "Just interested. I haven't gone to church for about thirty years."

Rather than trying to convince Stephen that he needed our church or any church, I said, "Why do you think so many people are exiting rather than entering churches? Are there any big deal-breaking questions that caused you to despair of organized religion because the churches didn't have answers to those questions?"

Stephen responded that he'd like to take some time to put them together "in a cogent list."

I said, "I would *love* to discuss these questions, because I think about this a lot too. And if by chance the LDS perspective shines any light on a question, I'll offer it to you." Stephen was amenable, and we set up a meeting early the next week.

At the next meeting I was quite stunned: Stephen had some very good questions—about the purpose of life, if there is one; what is God, if there is one; and so on. He said, "As I went through college and graduate school, the churches I attended just could not answer my questions. So I stopped going to church and have been looking for answers in philosophy and science instead. Frankly, they can't answer them any better than churches can."

We started at the top of Stephen's list. I asked questions about his first question, just to understand why it was important to him, and why he hadn't been impressed with the answers that others had offered. I then found and discussed answers to that question in the Book of Mormon.

I noticed that he crossed the first question off his list. "Why did you cross it off?" I asked.

"You answered it," he replied.

We then organized the subsequent lessons with the missionaries around the remaining questions on his list. When we scheduled a time for the zone leaders to interview Stephen for baptism, we listed all of the concepts, doctrines, and practices that are covered in the four lessons. We were delighted that we had covered every one of them, but in a sequence that answered Stephen's questions.*

Today, if someone asks me something about our church, I

Preach My Gospel teaches about asking questions in this fashion (see pages 21, 177, 183, 185, and 187).

don't tell him what *I* want *him* to know. Rather, I ask, "Do you have any questions about religious issues that you've been wondering about or that you haven't been able to get good answers to?" It turns out that there are a *lot* of people with questions. Most of them have given up on churches as a source of answers. As a consequence, even though they're interested in important questions, we categorize them as not interested in religion.

Explaining Ourselves through Questions

A friend once said, "I don't get it. Every Mormon I have met is a good, clear-minded person. What I don't get is how such good people believe in such a strange church!" I have concluded that the best way to resolve this paradox about us is by examining the *questions* that we typically ask in contrast to others, rather than comparing our answers to those that other churches offer. Though there is no "best" answer to a question like my friend posed, in the following paragraphs I'll recount how I used questions to explain our church to my friend.

I've never been to heaven, of course, I told him. But in trying to imagine what it is like, one metaphor that helps me is to imagine that God has constructed massive libraries in heaven. The shelves in these libraries are filled with books that are packed with truths, insights, and answers. Most of the books have never been checked out. Why, you might ask, are these stored in these libraries, rather than having have been distributed broadly to people on earth?

The reason is that people learn when they're ready to learn, not when we're ready to teach them. So if God directed a heavenly librarian to get the answer to question #23 off the shelf and send it down to some random person on earth, the answer would simply not be noticed. But when we ask a question, it is as if we put a Velcro pad in our brain where we need the answer. When the answer is then delivered, it sticks itself to the Velcro right where it is needed. The rule is this: Anybody on earth can check out any book—but the catch is that you need to ask the question first.

I told my friend that in the third century after Christ's death, the leaders of the early Christian Church essentially announced that God had given them all of the answers. And believing that they had received all the answers, there was no need to ask questions of God. When they stopped asking questions, revelation from heaven stopped. There was no need for prophets. These leaders essentially turned off the lights on the earth and plunged mankind into the dark ages.

Reformers like Luther, Wesley, and Calvin started asking questions again. But their questions were largely targeted to each other, debating interpretations of the answers that had been given centuries ago. They created churches that were differentiated one from another by the way they interpreted the answers. These men did enormous good in making the Bible available to people in their own languages and in explaining what it meant. But they did not revisit the basic conclusion of their early leaders—that all of the answers had been given to mankind.

I then told my friend that in 1820 in upstate New York, a fourteen-year-old boy, Joseph Smith, prayed to God, asking a simple question: Which, of all these churches, should he join? God and His Son Jesus Christ actually came down from heaven to personally give him the answer—that he should join none of them, because they were wrong. A simple boy asked a simple question and got a simple answer. And then they left.

For three more years, Joseph received no more answers from God because he essentially didn't ask any more questions. Then in 1823, at age seventeen, Joseph again prayed with a question—which in today's language essentially was this: "I'm sorry I've been out of touch, but it's not clear whether the ball is in my court or yours. Is there something you want me to do?" Immediately, an angel, Moroni, appeared and began answering Joseph's question about what God wanted him to do—and why.

Interestingly, however, the librarians in the heavenly libraries didn't announce over the loudspeaker system, "We've finally got our man down there. Let's empty the libraries and give that guy everything we've got!" Instead, over the next twenty years, Joseph Smith repeatedly asked questions of God about things he didn't understand. And God answered those questions step by step, clarifying questions about some of the answers that already been revealed and giving him additional truth. And to keep it all in perspective, God assured Joseph that He didn't plan to give him all the answers at that point—that there were many great and important things pertaining to the kingdom of God that He would give to them in the future—provided, of course, that they keep asking questions.

I explained to my new friend that while we refer to the work of Luther, Wesley, Calvin, and others as the *Reformation,* we call the story of Joseph Smith the beginning of the *Restoration* of the original church that Jesus established. In essence, it *restored questions to the earth,* which then elicited answers that man had previously not known. Because of this, we have learned much more about God's plan for us than is known among those who decided eighteen centuries ago that there were no more answers, no more questions. The salient difference between other churches and the LDS Church isn't a difference of orthodoxy versus unorthodoxy. Rather, it is the difference in the depth and breadth of understanding of God's plan for us. And this comes from the quality of the questions that are being asked. Oddly, the reason why some people frame Mormonism as "strange" is that we are in fact unique! We don't believe that God has ever given mankind all of the answers—and so we continue to ask.

"Got it," my friend noted. "But doesn't it bother you that it is predicated on a fourteen-year-old boy speaking with God and angels? To me, it is just an incredible story—as in *not a credible story*."

"Think about it this way," I responded. "Imagine that you were in heaven, wanting to give truth and insight and answers to mankind. Would you choose a spokesman for you on earth who truly believes that heaven already has given everything that is to be given? Or might you prefer instead someone whose mind is filled with questions, someone who is eager to get answers? Would you prefer someone who has advanced degrees from a divinity school, or a boy?"

I then summarized the background information about people whom God had called to become His prophets over time. There is information only for a few—including Enoch, Moses, Samuel, Saul, David, Jeremiah, and Amos. So I arrayed these stories on an oral spreadsheet of sorts, with these headings at the top of the columns: How old was he? What was his reaction to the call from God to be His prophet? Did the prophet know much about God or His plan for mankind at the time of his call? What, if known, was his profession or his educational background?

This arrayed a stunning pattern. All but one were young boys at the time they were called. Each was taken by total surprise, and some tried to convince God that He had asked the wrong man. Most were shepherds; they knew little about God or about what He had previously taught to earlier prophets. God then fundamentally changed them into powerful orators and leaders.

I then said, "Look at the pattern. The assertion that God and angels appeared to a simple, uneducated boy in the 1820s and called him to be His prophet to the world is the single most credible event in the history of religion in the last eighteen centuries. God had access to the best in the world. Why would He choose a simple boy?"

My friend answered, "I guess it is because he would ask a lot of questions."

What makes the LDS Church so different? Questions have been restored to the earth. As a church and as individuals we know much more about God's plan for us than is available for those who have been told that the "libraries" above were emptied of answers and padlocked centuries ago. Our story is not just credible. It is true.

Because God gives answers when we ask questions, it is a good way to do missionary work. People will learn when they are ready to learn, not when we are ready to teach them. Discovering what questions are on people's minds about religion helps me see that I actually am surrounded by many more people who are religious than I had imagined—because they have questions.*

---

*As an aside, one of the things I love about our church is the continued importance of asking good questions. We are urged at every level of the Church to question whether there is a better way of building the kingdom of God (see D&C 58:26–29). The phrase, "We believe that He will yet reveal many great and important things pertaining to the Kingdom of God" (Articles of Faith 1:9) does not have an expiration date on the package.

CHAPTER 3

Ask for Help When the Winds of Prosperity Blow

Many have noted that when people live in troubled circum-stances that *compel* them to be humble, they are more prone to listen to the gospel of Jesus Christ (see Alma 32). Because these are the people who tend to accept the gospel, the Lord noted that the restored gospel would be built on the shoulders of the weak and simple of the earth (see D&C 1:19–22).

One reason why our missionary work goes well among the humble people of the earth is that we, as a Church, are a helping, giving people. We invite such people into the Church by explaining how much the gospel helps us and demonstrating that it will help them, too.

Conducting missionary work among the prosperous of the earth, however, often requires a different mind-set. The principle is this: On occasion those who are in comfortable circumstances feel the need for a church affiliation. Most of the time, however, we will do better with this group if we can convey how desperately those of us in the Church need their help.

Though this idea seems paradoxical at first reading, it reflects a

35

fundamental causal mechanism of conversion that the Savior articulated: "For whosoever will save his life shall lose it; but whosoever shall lose his life for my sake and the gospel's, the same shall save it" (Mark 8:35).

In other words, we need to give the chance to lose their lives for the sake of the gospel not just to the humble of the earth, but to prosperous people too. Even though many prosperous, comfortable people don't feel like they need religion, almost all of them have a need to help other people.

Let me give you an example to illustrate this principle in action. I grew up in Rose Park, a wonderful neighborhood near downtown Salt Lake City. When I was a little boy my dad home taught a man named Phillip Strong. Phil had been baptized as a boy, but he hated the Church. Every month, my faithful father would take me or one of my brothers as his home teaching companion to make his visits. We would knock on Phillip's door. Phillip would come out on the porch and command my dad to get off his property and "Never come back or I'll call the police." But every month my faithful dad would knock on the door, only to be told again to get off.

One year in November, a wind-driven rainstorm came through Salt Lake. It was so strong that it blew off a chunk of the roof from a main building on Welfare Square. Someone called my dad, who was in our bishopric, to see if he could get a group of men to go to Welfare Square and fix the problem. So my dad left work early and went door to door, asking for volunteers. Most people said they would go. Then he came to Phillip Strong's house. It turns out Phillip Strong was an experienced tradesman. My dad passed his house and went to the next house. But then my dad stopped and said, "No, I've got to ask Phillip Strong."

He knocked on the door and, as happened each month, was

told to get off the porch. But Dad said, "Phillip, I don't want you to come to church. I need your help." He explained the problem and said, "I've got a group of people, but you are the one who knows how to fix problems like this. Can you come and just supervise this project?"

Phillip Strong agreed to come.

The men went up about 5:00 P.M. They had to illuminate the site. Rain was still coming down and the winds were very strong. They worked until 11:00 P.M. on that freezing roof. My dad said every time he drove another nail in the tar paper he felt like he was putting a nail into Phillip's spiritual coffin because the assignment was so miserable.

But when they climbed down from the roof, Phillip put an arm around my dad's shoulder and said, "I haven't felt this good in twenty years." And two weeks later Phillip Strong showed up to church. That was the beginning of his reactivation. The number of people in Rose Park that Phillip Strong and his family eventually brought into the Church, strengthening their faith, was extraordinary, truly extraordinary.

Consider the difference made by a shift in approach. Phil had regularly commanded my dad to get off the porch when the proposal was "Phil, you need the Church." But when the pitch was "Phillip, the Church needs you," instantly he said yes.

In the following pages I have recounted experiences that my friends, family members, and I have had as we have followed this principle. The stories appear in a different typeface to help convey the fact that they come from a variety of narrators. I recount them in the hope that they will help you see how badly you actually need the help of your friends who are not yet members of the Church, and how eager they are to help you. I have referred to the protagonist in each story as "I," whether it is my personal story or the story of another. The reasons for that approach are, first, some protagonists wanted to disguise proprietary information in the story, and second, I want to inspire you to think, as you read the stories, "This is my story! *I* can do this!"

Almost every calling that we undertake in the Church can be reframed as a missionary opportunity when we invite people who are not yet members of the Church to join with us in serving the Lord. And we can do it with confidence that, just as we feel the Spirit when we serve, our friends can feel the same Spirit—and realize that despite their prosperity, there has been something missing from their lives.

I hope that these experiences will help you visualize the wide range of things you can do.

Jim, Like It or Not, This Is the Mormon Church

I was the home teacher to an elderly woman in our ward. On a Saturday in July we experienced the worst of Boston's weather: The temperature was nearly 100 degrees F., and the humidity was above 90 percent. It was miserable. I decided that I had better visit Julia to be sure that she was okay. When I went into her home, I exclaimed to Julia, who had lost her sense of smell, "Something has died in this house! It smells awful." We followed the smell into her basement, where we saw the problem. The prior Christmas, her son who lived in Florida had shipped a case of grapefruit to his mother. Julia had put the case into an old refrigerator in her basement and then had forgotten that it was there. A bit later she heard an advertisement suggesting that unused appliances should be turned off. So Julia went right down and unplugged the refrigerator. Over the subsequent months the fruit had rotted, and the mold was everywhere. "Julia, we need to get this out of your house and get it to the dump," I told her.

I went home and phoned through the ward list, but nobody was available. Desperate, I asked a nonmember neighbor, Jim, to help. Several times previous to this I had asked Jim whether he might be interested to learn a bit about our wonderful church, but Jim had always kindly deflected my invitations. But to this call for help, he readily responded.

Not only was it hot and humid that day, but the task took *two hours* of *hard* work. The old fridge was *heavy*—made of cast iron, as best we could tell. It was wider than Julia's rickety basement staircase, which had two right-angle turns in it. So we had to take off the railings, and with WD-40 we got the door off the fridge. Soon our clothes were soaked with perspiration. When we reached the first turn in the staircase and had balanced the fridge on the landing, Jim said, "So, tell me about the Mormon church."

Mopping my brow, I responded, "Frankly, Jim, like it or not, this is the Mormon church." I then explained how home teaching worked, noted how much this sister needed us, and illustrated how our own home teacher helped our family. I also told him that because graduate students and their families were moving in and out of our area all the time, our family was often helping someone load or unload a rental truck.

Jim was incredulous. "At our church we just listen to the sermon and go home. I have no idea who might need *my* help, and there is no way that they might know whether I needed *their* help. I like this kind of thing. The next time one of you Mormons needs help, will you ask me?"

Although I had tried to engage Jim in discussions about religion in the past, Jim was uninterested. But he was interested in opportunities to help others. Jim felt something that he had rarely felt in his church, and he subsequently accepted our invitation to take the missionary discussions.

Tom, Who Didn't Know That He Was Interested

Several years ago I became acquainted with Tom Singleton and invited him to begin playing in our 7:00 A.M. Saturday basketball game at our ward building. Tom began coming, and he seemed to enjoy the camaraderie that we enjoyed there. I decided Tom was a good candidate for the missionary discussions, so I asked him if he would like to take them. Tom's response was, "If I say I'm not interested, will you still let me play ball?" I said, "Of course," and Tom responded in his typically unvarnished way, "Good. I'm not interested."

Tom kept playing with us. He seemed to be enjoying the game with the guys in the ward so much that I decided a few months later to invite him again to come to our home and learn a bit about what made Mormons tick.

"Did the rules change?" Tom asked.

"What rules?" was my response.

"You told me that I didn't have to become a Mormon in order to play ball."

"No, you don't need to become a Mormon, Tom. We love having you come. I just thought that you'd like to know something that all of these guys share in common," I said.

"Thanks. But I'm really not interested."

At about that time, a new missionary was assigned to our ward. It always had been a hard place to find people to teach, and as a consequence this young missionary had never taught anything beyond the first discussion in the three months he had been serving. So, after a basketball game a few weeks later, I pulled Tom Singleton aside. I said, "Tom, I know you have no interest in becoming a Mormon. But I wonder if you could help me. Just like I was a missionary for the Church in Korea, young missionaries have been assigned to work here. They are supposed to learn how to teach a set of lessons to people who are interested in learning about our church. But the problem is that everyone in this area seems to be a hardened Catholic like you. *Nobody* seems interested. Without anybody to teach, they just haven't been able to learn these lessons, but they need to be ready, just in case they run into somebody who is curious. Is there any way these guys could come to your house and just let them practice teaching these lessons to you? I want you to give them a hard time—really make it as realistic a practice as you can." Tom accepted.

I told the missionaries what the deal was—that Tom wasn't interested in our church, but that he had offered to help them practice their teaching. I told them to teach in as sincere and realistic a way as possible. I went to the first lesson just to be sure they followed the rules. At the end of the first lesson, the junior companion pulled out a copy of the Book of Mormon and offered it to Tom and his wife, Ann, saying, "Would you read this book?" To our great surprise, they accepted it and said they would. They did, and they were baptized.

When my invitation centered on how the Church would interest them, Tom wasn't interested. But when I asked for help, Tom said, "Sure." He and his wife have become wonderful members of our ward.

The Eye of a Fly, a Welded Beam of Steel, and Alcohol

When I served as priests quorum adviser, we reserved the third Tuesday of every month as a "career night," an event where we met a member of the ward in his or her place of employment. Those individuals would then explain or show what their professions entailed.

At that time, one of my company's premier scientists, Mark, seemed to have a grudge against Mormons, and he would find a way to ridicule the Church in any conversation.

On the Sunday before a scheduled career night, the ward member who had volunteered to introduce us to his profession said that he couldn't do it because he had to leave town unexpectedly on company business. So the next day I told Mark about our career nights and that our next host could not do it. "Mark, sorry to ask this with so little notice," I said, "but is there any way that you could introduce materials science to our boys tomorrow night if we brought them here to your lab?"

"I'd be happy to do that," was Mark's reply. "What time can you get them here, and when do you need to finish to get them home on time?"

The next evening was perhaps the most engaging activity in the history of our youth program. Mark was an expert in the use of the electron microscope, and he had learned that when he covered the specimen he was working on with a thin film of gold, it maximized the clarity of the image. So Mark had killed a housefly and sputtered it with a film of gold. We spent two hours studying the eye of a housefly through an electron microscope. Every priest left Mark's lab with the resolve to become a scientist.

Another man I met ran a welding shop. I asked him to teach my priests how to weld. When we arrived I found that he had cut steel rods to standard lengths, and he gave a set of these rods to each boy. He had purposefully left himself one kit short so that he could teach the boys how to cut rods of steel with an acetylene torch. He then helped each boy weld his rods together into a bar stool to take home. They were *really* cute stools, and these seventeen-year-olds were just beaming with pride as we left. When I tried to pay my friend for the cost of the steel, he wouldn't take the money, and instead thanked me for being so interested in his work.

Another time, I asked a policeman to tell the boys what his job was like. Among other things, he took them through the process for arresting drivers suspected of being intoxicated. He brought a bottle of whiskey and took a swallow (unusual in our church) so that the boys could smell his breath and see how quickly it could be measured.

Without exception, these activities that my nonmember friends managed were of especially high quality. They had never been asked to do this sort of thing before, and they seemed to feel complimented that the boys were interested in their professions. None of these friends has yet joined our church, but each of them gained an understanding of the essence of our religion *much* more deeply than if they had just read something.

The Best Samaritan

Some time ago I called my friend Susan, who is not a member of our church, and asked, "I teach a class of nine-year-olds at our church. In two weeks I've got to teach them one of the most important lessons of the year, about the good Samaritan. Susan, you are the best example of a good Samaritan I have ever known. Is there any way you can help me prepare and teach this lesson?" Susan felt that she didn't merit such praise, but she said that she'd be happy to help.

After Susan and I met to plan the lesson, I said, "One of the practices in our church is that when we deliver a talk or teach a lesson, we close by giving our testimony, or a statement of our personal belief, about the topic. So I will probably express a simple testimony of my personal feelings about the principle of the good Samaritan. Don't feel like you need to do this too, but if you feel inclined, I'm sure it will touch some of the kids."

Susan replied, "If you think it will help the kids, I'll try to do it."

The lesson went beautifully. After I bore my testimony, Susan tearfully described how she felt whenever she helped another person. When we were putting the room in order after the children had left, Susan thanked me for the chance to help, and then said, "I never show my emotions like I did just now. And I've never felt inside the way that I feel now. Does this happen to you too?"

"Yes," I responded. "What you feel is the Spirit of God. It is the way that God tells you that what you just said is true."

Susan offered, "If you *ever* need anyone to help you with another lesson, would you please let me do it? I've never felt like this before!"

Sacrament Bread Coordinator

Several months after moving into our big ward, I was called to be the sacrament bread coordinator. I just needed to bring a loaf of bread on Sunday. Period. I didn't realize how badly I needed to feel needed—and this call told me that in fact I wasn't needed!

A while later I heard someone at church say that every calling, in one way or another, can be transformed into a missionary calling. It made me wonder, "Is there any way that I could transform the calling of sacrament bread coordinator into a missionary calling?"

After a few minutes of thinking, I said to myself, "I hate to bake bread, right? Maybe I could make a list of women who are not active or not yet members of the Church, who like to cook. I can tell them: 'I have this calling in the Church, and I want to put my whole soul into it. I don't want to just bring bread, I want to take bread that I have made myself, just as a signal to the Lord that I really take the sacrament seriously. Is there a way that you could teach me how to make the best loaf of bread in the world—something that I could be proud of when I take the sacrament this Sunday?'"

I decided to give this a try. Because bread dough needs to rise, this required about three hours every Saturday. Not a single woman turned me down, and they brought their best recipes. I quickly became a gourmet connoisseur of breads. But more important, it gave us three hours to talk about a lot of things, including the gospel.

Packing a U-Haul

A group of six of us in the ward were working early on a Saturday morning to load the Simpsons' furniture and possessions into their U-Haul truck. They were moving to another state, and we were going to miss them. As the morning progressed, it was clear that the Simpsons had a lot more stuff than we expected.

Several of us had other commitments later that morning, and I was wondering how we were going to get the packing done before we had to leave. I then noticed that Dave, the Simpsons' neighbor in their duplex, was standing on his porch watching us, smoking. I went over, introduced myself, and asked, "Any way you could help us pack that truck? We're running late."

"Sure," Dave responded as he put out his cigarette. Dave proved to be a great addition, and he helped us finish things in time. When the work was done, as we each shook Dave's hand in gratitude for his help, Dave asked, "Who are you guys, anyway?"

I told him about the LDS Church and how we all tried to help each other when things like that arose. Then I asked, "If you ever have some time and interest, could I come back and tell you a little about us? It really is a great group of people."

"Sure. I don't have a lot going on, so anytime would be fine with me."

Dave subsequently was baptized, along with his children, and he later became a temple ordinance worker.

A Fixture for Pamphlets

I decided we needed to have a rack on the wall at church that was regularly replenished with pamphlets about the Church that the members could give to their friends. My neighbor was a scientist whose hobby was to make furniture in his garage shop. So I asked him if he could help me think through what a pamphlet rack might look like. He asked if I would give him samples of the pamphlets so that he could visualize a rack for them. I gave him a set, and he spent several hours studying them. The next evening he knocked on our door to show me his drawings. The rack that he envisioned looked beautiful.

I said, "Mel, I hadn't meant to ask you to do drawings like this for me. I just wanted you to give me some general guidance. I'm so grateful that you would do this, but please, let me take it from here."

Mel replied, "Don't you like my work?" He asked me a few questions and then said, "Let me keep these for another day. I'd just like to change a few details."

The next evening Mel knocked on our back door. In his hands were all the components for the rack, cut from oak.

"Mel, this is way beyond what I had imagined," I protested. "You shouldn't do this. But oh my gosh, these are just elegant. Could you let me take it out of your hands? I'm sure I can assemble them together."

Mel showed me how they fit together, asked a few questions, and then said, "I want to change a few things first, so I'll bring them over tomorrow."

The next day Mel appeared at the back door with the entire rack assembled, glued, sanded, and hand-finished with oil. It truly was beautiful in design and fabrication.

When I expressed my wonderment for his artistry, Mel asked, "Can we install it in the church tonight?" I protested that I had imposed on his time enough, but Mel retorted, "Look, I know how to fasten things like this into plaster walls. If you don't do it right, some kid is going to rip this off the wall. Come with me so you can learn a few things."

By 9:00 that night we had a beautiful rack in the foyer of the chapel, filled with missionary pamphlets. I was just stunned by what Mel had done. I then gave him a tour of the building. At the end we just sat down in the chapel. I told him a bit of history about the building, and then discussed his questions about our church.

Help with My Talk

A few months ago I was asked to speak in sacrament meeting. I am the worst public speaker in the ward: I just freeze at the pulpit. But this time I asked my friend Megan to help me. She isn't a member of the Church, but at PTO meetings she always seems to be self-assured when she speaks. So I called her and asked if she could help me give a great sacrament meeting talk. Megan gladly said she could help. After I wrote a draft of my talk, Megan came to my place so I could practice delivering the talk. Megan gave a lot of feedback on the substance of the talk, particularly on issues that weren't clear to her as a nonmember. And she gave great feedback on my delivery. Several days later she listened again to my delivery. She was *very* complimentary—I'm sure she was just trying to build my confidence.

When I thanked Megan for her support and help, she asked, "Can I come to the service so that I can witness the real thing?" I was surprised, but said, "I'd be honored!"

At the end of the meeting, Megan said, "Great job. Truly, great job! I had no idea that the Mormon church is like this. If I can help you with your next one, would you please call?"

How Broadly Do These Principles Apply?

Here's what these experiences from a broad range of members have taught me. When our invitations to others to investigate the Church emphasize doctrine, or focus on how much the Church can help them, we often do not connect with what prosperous people are looking for. But in many people who are satisfied with their lives, the light of Christ continues to create a deep need inside to help others. We need to help all God's children find ways to lose their lives for the sake of the Savior. This follows the thoughts and the ways of God.

NOTES

Inviting others to help us with our work in the Church helps them feel needed, to realize that we have a lot in common, and to feel the Spirit. When these feelings come, many people then realize that something *has* been missing from their lives. When we help others to do God's will, they learn far more about what the Church and the Spirit feels like than they ever could through a conversation or from attending a ward social.

Because of the structure of our church, opportunities to help others are in our faces 24–7. We take these opportunities for granted. But most other people just don't know where to find such opportunities. They are comfortable with their lives, they live among similarly comfortable people, and they attend churches that don't provide such opportunities. We don't realize how fortunate we are.

When my friends have a great experience helping me, I then follow my practice described in the previous chapter: I decouple my friendship with them from my invitation to learn more about the gospel by asking them to promise that they will say no if they're not interested. If I don't do that, then they might surmise that I had an ulterior motive in asking for help. I need to be sure that they know that I truly needed and was grateful for their help.

Several years ago I talked about the principles presented in this chapter with Gary Crittenden, the president of the Yorktown New York Stake at that time, and his stake and ward leaders. They concluded that the ward mission plans of each ward in the stake would focus on two things. First, they asked members to get involved in community organizations so that they would know many more people in their communities. Second, they committed each member to invite someone who was not a member of our church to join with them in serving in the Church. This stake covers some of the wealthiest communities in the world, and its baptism totals historically were the lowest of the stakes in the New York North Mission.

When the members began to ask people to serve side-by-side with them in the Church, however, the number of people baptized the next year tripled, putting the stake as the *top* stake in the mission in baptisms—even beyond stakes whose populations were living in circumstances that compelled them to be humble.

I testify that God has not restricted the privilege of feeling the Spirit to active members of the Church. Those who are not members of our church, as well as those who are less active, can feel the same Spirit we feel when we give them the chance to lose their lives for the sake of the Savior and His gospel.

NOTES

CHAPTER 4

Share the Truth at Work in a Proud and Confident Way

NOTES

Work comprises the venues in which we meet and interact with most of the people in our lives who are not of our faith.* Most of us spend a lot of time "at work." And yet it is broadly believed that talking about the Church with others at work is awkward and often not appropriate. This chapter has two simple purposes. First, I want to show how critical it is that we learn how to share the gospel at work. Of all the battles in the war that we are fighting against Satan, this is a big one—and in many ways we are retreating from this battle, ceding this venue to the adversary. My second purpose is to review the obvious: The way that Heber C. Kimball did missionary work—standing on a box on the public square and giving a sermon—is one way to do the work. But it is not the only way. There are other ways to be bold and direct in sharing the gospel that work much better at work.

Some will say after reading this chapter that "Clayton

---

*For brevity, I designate our professional pursuits, our study at school or college, and all of our work in community organizations as "at work."

Christensen can share the gospel at work because his life is very different from mine. He has become somewhat successful in his profession. Nobody will fire him if he talks about the Church at work. I'm in a very different situation, working my way up from the bottom. If I say some of the things Clay says, I'll get fired—or at a minimum they'll label me as someone who is different."

It's hard to know whether indeed Clay is an unusual case. All I can say is that I have had four different careers: seven years as a graduate student, five years as a consultant, five years as an entrepreneur, and now twenty years in academia. In each I was not prominent or successful in the beginning, and in some of them I left those professions in obscurity, too. But in each profession I have tried to share the gospel with as many people as I could, regardless of my position. In every job, I've tried to learn what works and what doesn't in sharing the gospel, so that I might be a better missionary. This is what I offer to you in this chapter.

I say with conviction at the outset that when Christ said, "But seek ye first the kingdom of God, and his righteousness; and all these things shall be added unto you" (Matthew 6:33), He meant what He said. I have felt—literally—that my personal abilities have grown beyond what my normal abilities could otherwise have been because I have sought to contribute to building the kingdom of God—even while I have been at work.

A Paradox Framed by Satan

Because work is where we can most readily meet and engage in conversations about the gospel, Satan is *very* committed to stop this from happening. To convey how Satan stands in our way, I'll start this chapter by recounting a "conversation" I had with Satan or one of his colleagues. Don't be alarmed—every time Satan tempts us, we're having a conversation of sorts, as he speaks to our spirit trying to convince us to do something wrong, and our spirit says in turn that we are not going to do what he suggested. I have, with apologies to the renowned Christian author C. S. Lewis, attempted to replicate the style of his wonderful book *The Screwtape Letters*. It is a "conversation" in our minds that occurs many times every day between members of the Church and the demon who is trying to convince us not to do what is right. I'll give this particular adversary the name "Sharpfork."

"Wait a minute," I thought to Sharpfork. "What you're telling me is that when I'm at work, I should not talk to anybody about my beliefs. It isn't politically correct, and people will be offended if I do. Religion must be a private affair. Do I have it right?"

"Clay, you have it exactly right," Sharpfork responded.

"But Jesus Christ wants me to share His gospel with everybody—including those at work!"

"Of course He wants this," Sharpfork retorted. "Who wouldn't?"

"Well, the problem is this," I complained. "Suppose that I follow your advice, and don't talk to anyone about the gospel at work. For sixty hours each week (five days times twelve hours, including commuting), you are putting missionary work out of bounds. Right? The problem then is that on Saturday I'm supposed to spend that time with my family, and they are all Mormons. And on Sunday I spend my time with my family and at church, where everybody is a Mormon. So what you're saying to me is that except for those seven days every week, I can share the gospel with others. Do I have it right?"

"Exactly," Sharpfork answered. "That is the beauty of it!"

Although most of us have not framed it as such, almost all of us have had this conversation—and this, in turn, causes us to feel that we face a paradox, knowing that sharing the gospel with others would please the Lord, and yet not seeing a way to do it.

If the prohibition against talking about religion at work were a preference of executives, then different companies would have different views on it. And if the injunction against religious discussions were based in a worry that they would hurt employees' productivity, then discussions about other beliefs—like politics, ethnic differences, sports, and so on—would also be viewed as detracting from productivity in the workplace. The fact that the prohibition applies only to religion, and that the ban on religious discussion seems to be in force at nearly every workplace, leads me to believe that this particular cultural belief is the work of Satan. I see no other plausible explanation.

Why does it matter to Satan what we talk about when we're at work or school? It is a continued attack in the war that Satan initiated in heaven against God's plan of free agency. Having lost the first round in the premortal existence, Satan has a different strategy for foiling free agency on the earth. For God's plan to be fulfilled, each of us needs to be confronted with the chance to choose between good and evil; otherwise we could not act for ourselves. As Lehi noted: "Wherefore, the Lord God gave unto man that he should act for himself. Wherefore, man could not act for himself save it should be that he was enticed by the one *or the other*" (2 Nephi 2:16; emphasis added).

Knowing that God's plan required that Satan be allowed to tempt us, how can Satan use this to his advantage in his continued war against free agency? He simply needs to convince the members of The Church of Jesus Christ of Latter-day Saints that it is awkward and politically incorrect to talk about God's plan with others at work. If Satan achieves this objective, then many, many of God's children will be enticed by one (Satan) and *not* the other (members), and it will be harder for people to choose the right.

Satan often appears to be winning this round of his war against free agency. Gary Lawrence and I independently have observed that far less than 10 percent of the Saints of God are inviting their neighbors, classmates, and work colleagues to learn of the gospel of Jesus Christ. People can't act for themselves if the Latter-day Saints close their mouths, and this is exactly what Satan is accomplishing. This is a big deal.

Illustrations of How to Share the Gospel at Work

Recognizing that the fear of talking about our beliefs is a construct of Satan has given me courage. I acknowledge Satan's threats about discussing beliefs at work—and you should too. But do not be deterred. What I have learned in this process is that there are two fundamentally different ways to be a missionary: through word and through deed. The first is to explain what the gospel is and how it has been restored to the earth. The second is to explain the gospel by overtly *using* it to solve important problems at work. Both ways give you chances to testify.

By Word

When we use the words *share the gospel,* our instincts often are actually to *share* things—homemade cookies, pass-along cards, copies of the Book of Mormon, and so on. This mode of sharing has been hard for me to initiate at work because it disrupts rather than fits into the flow of my work. This way of sharing at work brings attention to the actions themselves and can actually even detract from the content of the gospel.

A better way I've found to share by word is to put my testimony and my life story online. It fits with the flow of work more easily because I can say it on my time, and others can read and think about it on their time. If I then follow the principle discussed in chapter 2 above, to mix into every conversation religious and Mormon words, I can refer my coworkers to what I have said online.

Many times every week colleagues respond to my use of Mormon words by saying, "I believe in God too" or "I'm a believer too."

I then can respond, "Aren't you glad that we believe in God? I sure feel sorry for those who don't. In fact, a bit ago I summarized my current thoughts about faith and put them on my website. Here is the URL, in case you're interested. I'd love to get your feedback. Have you ever done something like this?" . . . and so on.

As a general rule, a large majority of people at work actually believe in God. The minority who have decided that there is no God or that discussions about religion are out of bounds have sometimes imposed the opinion of the few upon the will of the many. I have found, as a consequence, that if I have the courage to use religious words in my language at work—and do it in a normal, matter-of-fact way—I actually free many of my colleagues from the same shackles that originally had constrained me.

Within the last year, two presidents of significant universities in the Boston area independently thanked me for speaking about God openly. Both described truly feeling isolated by the vocal atheists in their institutions who declare that faith and religion are out of bounds.

Even at a secular institution like mine, I have found so many who are eager to discuss their faith in God that I literally could spend hours every day with just a fraction of those who are anxious to discuss the gospel of Jesus Christ. In most instances this method of sharing the gospel has worked because I could initiate our first communications when it fit for me, and the interested parties have been able to listen when it fits for them. Then it doesn't disrupt things at work because we know some of the issues that we have in common.

By Deed

The second way to share the gospel at work is to *use* the gospel explicitly to solve problems that we encounter. Almost always these circumstances entail teaching others. Some happen when we are standing in front of a class. More often, however, teaching entails one-on-one explanation of how to do something, how to be more successful, how to solve a problem, to communicate better, and so on. Most teachers, in a didactic way, give their "students" a step-by-step checklist of what needs to be done. Good teachers often then illustrate the instructions with stories. In fact, a key reason why the Savior was such a magnificent teacher is that He used metaphors, stories, and parables to illustrate the key points. Mustard seeds, sparrows, the good Samaritan, and the prodigal son all help us visualize what He wants us to do. As a result, whenever I'm in a teaching situation, I try to find a story about something that we do or have done in the Church to illustrate what we need to do at work.

Following are three personal experiences to show how you can use the gospel to address common challenges.

Use Home Teaching in Employee Plans

Several years ago I was on a consulting assignment with a huge European company that makes branded personal care products.

It employs hundreds of thousands of employees, and its products are in most homes in the world. The particular issue that we were wrestling with was this: New, incremental products whose plans promised results within two years or so always received a higher priority than products that might be more stable and important over their lifespan. The company simply could not make investments in innovative products that would bear fruit only over a longer term.

A key culprit, we decided, was a system that identified "high potential" employees in the company: smart, capable, committed junior managers in a sophisticated, competitive system. These were essentially "anointed" as those who would lead the corporation ten and twenty years in the future. To prepare them, a plan was established for each of these high-potential managers—a plan that would send them in two-year stints as managers in subsidiary companies in nations around the world. These rotations entailed assignments in marketing, new product management, manufacturing, finance, and other areas. The hope was that through this sequence of assignments, the high-potential employees could develop a sophisticated sense of how the corporation operated around the world and how the functions and components fit together into the whole.

When I asked my host how the sequence of assignments was determined, he answered that about eighteen months into an assignment, their superiors convened to rank these junior managers according to what they had accomplished in the current assignment. There were "plum" assignments and pedestrian ones. The high-potential managers who did best in the current assignment got the best assignments in the next round. This meant that within eight to ten years, five or so managers were clear leaders in the class

NOTES

and had so much momentum that they were moving farther ahead of the pack in the race that would determine the next CEO.

"There's your answer," I said to my host. "If there is a great innovation that won't bear fruit within eighteen months, no high-potential manager would propose it. On his watch in the assignment, his record would show costs that had been incurred but little to show for them within the eighteen-month window. So the high-potential system penalizes investments on long-term possibilities and rewards short-term mentality among your most promising managers." This was a sobering revelation to my host.

I then asked, "So every year you select from the entering 'class' the high-potential managers. What happens to the rest? Do they have potential, and if so, how do you cultivate it?"

The answer was obvious: These have potential too. But he maintained that with hundreds of thousands of employees, they could not establish and monitor a personal development plan for all of them. "So everybody else needs to sink or swim. Occasionally one of them does so well that we admit them into the high-potential pool late."

I said, "I have an idea for you, as a mechanism for developing and monitoring a career plan for many more of the hundreds of thousands of employees. As you might know, I'm a member of the LDS or Mormon church, and we have exactly your problem but at an even larger scale. We don't have any professional ministers who operate the Church. We teach and care for one another. But this means that we all need to learn how to lead, and learn who needs what kind of help or development. One way we do this is through programs called home teaching and visiting teaching."

We spent the next four hours talking about how these programs work in theory and in practice in the Church and how a similar program might be implemented in this company. The concept: Every employee could have two others who had responsibility to keep their fingers on his or her pulse to be sure that everything was working well. We decided to call these "companions" and "home teachers" in the company, for short. Importantly, each companionship would formulate a career plan for two or three other coworkers that they were assigned to watch over. Most employees had no ambitions to become the next CEO. But almost everyone wanted to learn, grow, achieve, and get more responsibility and recognition. Each companionship would develop a plan for those that they home taught, to help them achieve these things. The plan could be given to the Human Resources (HR) office, and every month each companionship would report back to the head of HR how well the plan for each employee was working.

This was one of the most exciting discussions I have ever had about the Church. My host was extraordinarily insightful. At one point I asked him, "Who would you assign as the home teacher to the CEO? The executive vice president?"

"No," he replied. "One would be a salesman. The other would be a scientist in new product development."

At another point in the discussion we were looking at an organizational chart of the Church, with its headquarters, stakes, and wards. My host pointed to the box labeled "Elders Quorum President" and asked, "What does this guy do?"

I responded, "What they uniformly do well is organize crews of members to move people with U-Haul trucks in and out of their apartments in the spring and fall in Boston. Beyond that, it's pretty variable."

My host then wrote next to this Elders Quorum box, "Chief Human Relations Officer." He said, "I actually think I might implement home teaching in my part of the company. This is a great idea. I'm not sure that I want to be called 'Bishop' rather than 'CEO,' however."

I responded, "If you do this, you should then get baptized into the Mormon church so that you can help us make the program work better."

"I might," he replied. "I just might."

I did not set out to explain the Church to my host. Rather, I used the principles of the gospel of Jesus Christ to help him solve a problem. He learned more about the Church than I ever imagined he would, and at several points in the discussion he and I felt the Spirit guiding us to see and understand things that normally we could not have seen. What this CEO felt and saw is that the gospel actually works.

Counseling Jack

My second story is one of counseling. This occurred when Jack, a former student of mine, visited me in hopes that I could help him get a job. Seven years earlier the CEO of his company had retired, and Jack, as vice president, had felt that he would be the next CEO. But Wendy, whom he had never met, was brought in from the outside and put in charge instead.

Wendy was driven to maximize profits—and she cut expenses to the bone to do this. This included literally zeroing out their entire budget for developing next-generation products. Her relentless focus on costs resulted in a sixfold increase in profits. Wendy's track record of restoring companies to prosperity was broadly viewed as brilliant, and three years after taking the CEO position, she was lured away by a very attractive salary to run a bigger company. Wendy's timing was uncanny, because the next quarter Jack's company announced that revenues had dropped by nearly 10 percent, the result of Wendy's not having invested in new growth products. The board asked Jack to take the helm, with a charge to get the company growing again. Doing this entailed building an R&D capability again, but it was too little, too late. The company's stock price tumbled; the company was acquired; and the CEO of the acquiring company told Jack that he was no longer needed. Hence, Jack needed my help.

These injustices consumed Jack. He was mad at the board for hiring Wendy instead of him. He was *very* angry with Wendy, of course, because Jack had essentially been punished for Wendy's mismanagement, even while Wendy was rewarded.

"Clay, I need a job," Jack said. "In every interview, they assume that the company tanked under my watch. I try to explain that it was the fault of the prior CEO, but so far, I just can't escape this legacy."

I said, "In listening, Jack, I *feel* it. You really are *mad*. What I worry about is that some of the people that you're interviewing with likely will feel it too, because they can't gauge who you really are. They might be thinking, *Is this just an angry man? How is he going to work in our company?*"

I continued, "I try to read the scriptures every morning when I get here, just to be sure my head is screwed on right for the day ahead. I read something just a few days ago that might help. Would you mind reading this out loud? It is in our modern scriptures."

I then pulled my scriptures off my shelf and opened to D&C 64:8–10: "My disciples, in days of old, sought occasion against one another and forgave not one another in their hearts; and for this evil they were afflicted and sorely chastened. Wherefore, I say unto you, that ye ought to forgive one another; for he that forgiveth not his brother his trespasses standeth condemned before the Lord; for there remaineth in him the greater sin. I, the Lord, will forgive whom I will forgive, but of you it is required to forgive all men."

"It looks to me like you're blaming lots of people for what has happened," I said. "And it is true that they caused the trouble. But what part of the problem are you going to solve by being mad at everyone?"

"Clay, *somebody* ought to make things right. I was left with the problems Wendy created, and it derailed *my* career, not hers!" Jack responded.

I said, "Let me tell you about something that happened in my church a number of years ago. In a Scout troop that our church sponsored, the Scoutmaster abused twin twelve-year-old boys. When their mother told the bishop of the ward, he quickly met with the Scoutmaster, verified that it had happened, and then brought in the man's wife so that the Scoutmaster could confess to her what he had done. In subsequent weeks the man was excommunicated from the Church and was referred to government authorities, where he confessed to all that had happened.

"This was devastating to everyone concerned. Several friends urged his wife to divorce him. Instead, she forgave him. They moved to a different state, where they could start again.

"The mother of the twins, in contrast, was irate. 'If the bishop of the ward had been attuned to the Spirit, he never would have asked that man to be the Scoutmaster in the first place,' she complained. 'As long as he is bishop of the ward, I am not going to attend church again.' She would not allow her children to attend church either.

"After years had passed, I learned that in the town to which the Scoutmaster and his wife had moved, Church leaders determined that he had truly repented of his problems, and he was again baptized into the Church.

"When the mother of the twins learned of this, she announced that 'This does it. If they admit people like him into the Church, it cannot be guided by God.' She asked that her name and the names of her twins be taken off the membership records of the Church. She and her husband were subsequently divorced—the result, friends surmised, of her having become so bitter against everyone and everything."

I asked Jack, "Who were the winners and who were the losers in this story?"

The winner, Jack realized, was the wife of the Scoutmaster. Her family was stronger in every way because she could forgive and get to work solving the problems. "And the big loser?" I asked. Clearly, it was the mother of the twins. Her feelings of injustice still boil in her heart. Her marriage dissolved, and she and her boys are alienated from God.

I then read D&C 64:10 again aloud, and asked, "God's language is pretty clear here. He reserves for Himself the right to forgive or not forgive whomever He wants. But for us, it is a blanket requirement. There are no set asides, circumstances, or contingencies. We are to forgive everybody, all of the time. Why is God so dogmatic about forgiveness?" I asked.

Jack started to cry. "He has seen so many instances of people ruining their own lives when they will not forgive. God doesn't want this to happen to me." Jack then asked, "I came looking for a job, and you talked about God. Why?"

"I just do it when God can help us solve a problem," I responded. "I think that God truly is my Father—and yours. He wants to help you. I would be foolish if I didn't use the best concepts or ways of solving a problem."

Jack left with a spring in his step. He shortly found a great job and quickly wrote to ask me to write down the scripture we had read. "So I can tape it on my desk," he said. I did so, and I also sent him a triple combination, writing above my signature, "Just in case you ever need to screw your head on straight in the morning, read this."

Speaking with Love

My third example: A number of years ago, a number of students in my class at the Harvard Business School, for reasons that I could not figure out, truly did not enjoy the class. This was a new experience for me, as my courses had been quite popular with students year after year. I met with the disgruntled students individually and in groups, asking what I needed to change so that they felt they were learning well. Each person put her or his finger on a different aspect of my teaching or the curriculum that they didn't like. It added up to a mandate that I needed to do everything differently. What made it more complicated was that most of the other students seemed to be quite happy with the course.

I asked several more experienced members of our faculty to observe me teaching, in hopes that they could find something that I needed to change, but they didn't see anything that merited significant overhaul. I was *very* frustrated. Our students pay a lot to attend Harvard, and I have always wanted to give every student extraordinary value in every class.

In the midst of this, on a flight to Minneapolis I sat next to an elderly man who belonged to the Lakota Indian tribe. He was very wise. When he learned of my profession, he asked, "Is it fun to teach at Harvard?"

I responded that it normally was, but that particular semester was trying. I explained what was going on in this particular section of my course. After patiently listening to me, he said, "The reason this is happening is that you are not teaching with love. You always need to teach with love."

This was a profound comment that took me by complete surprise, as the concepts of teaching with love and the Harvard Business School case method probably had never been put together in any sort of free-association exercise prior to this. But I realized that I, in fact, wasn't dealing with these naysayers in the forgiving, loving way that Jesus had advised.

When I resumed teaching the next day, I remembered the man's wise words. I knelt in my office and prayed that God would help me to teach with love, that the students might be able to feel God's love for them emanating from me through the way that I taught. Within a few days the spirit of animosity just seemed to disappear in that class. It was replaced with a spirit of warmth, trust, and happiness, and many of the students in that group have remained close to me to this day. Many of them asked what happened in the class, and I told them of the wise counsel that I received. I told them that every day before class, I prayed that the Spirit of God would be in our class. One of them, Rob, joined the Church the next summer. Much of his motivation to seek out the Church, he reported, came from the spirit he felt in our class.

That day, and prior to each class I have taught since that time, I have followed that practice and knelt to ask God to help me in my teaching. I have subsequently expanded what I pray for every morning: that every person that I interact with that day will be able to feel my love for them and to feel God's love for them emanating from me. I continue to try to do this, and I am grateful to say that I am periodically successful in this effort. I have never been asked by anyone to stop being kind or to stop helping others feel loved. Because I try to use Mormon words in my normal conversations, everyone knows that these feelings are associated with our wonderful church.

Science, Academia, and Religion

One of the most intolerant climates for discussion about religion is among scientists and academics. Although they fashion themselves as the most fair and open-minded of all people, in my experience many in academia can actually be very biased and closed-minded against truth. Many people are cowed into believing that because some of the most erudite among us disparage religion, academia and religion are not compatible—that they actually cannot be employed in the same conversation. Many treat religion as a second-tier stepchild when juxtaposed with scientific and academic inquiry, and many of us therefore conclude that bringing religion up in politically correct conversations will cause others to think less of us.

I have decided that rather than framing such colleagues as intellectual *opponents,* I should instead view them as having been deceived by Satan, just like the rest of us often are. With this as my mind-set, I can frame my interactions with colleagues as if we are always on the same side of any divide.

Here is my logic. God did *not* say to us in the premortal existence, "Children, shortly you each are going down to earth, and I want you to be very careful. When you get there you're going to confront bodies of beliefs that they'll call *science* and *academia.* You will find these riddled with inconsistencies when compared to the truth about me, and the more you study, the more it will destroy your faith in me. So be *very* careful with science and academia: learn as little of those things as you can."

God did not say this.

The great scientist Henry Eyring taught this principle over and over: Truth, from whatever source makes it known, helps us to become more like God.

The evening before young Henry was going to leave home

to study engineering at the University of Arizona, his father, Ed Eyring, asked Henry to take a walk with him around the family's cattle ranch. He did not counsel Henry to learn selectively. Rather, he said, "In this church you don't have to believe anything that isn't true. You go over to the University of Arizona and learn everything that you can, and whatever is true is part of the gospel."*

The Restoration of the gospel allows us to categorize things by "truth vs. falsehood" instead of "science vs. religion." This has made me unafraid. It helps me to instinctively draw upon concepts from religion to solve problems in business and in academia, as readily as I draw upon academic concepts to solve these problems. Ed Eyring helped me see that there isn't a hierarchy of types of truth. Scientific and academic pursuits are not superior in any way to truth that we learn from religion, *and vice versa.* Correctly defined, there is inherently not a contradiction. If we observe that academia and science on the one side and religion on the other are inconsistent, then one or the other is wrong or incomplete, or they are both incomplete or both wrong. But truth cannot be inconsistent with truth. We are on solid ground as long as we are humbly searching for the truth.

~~

The experiences I've had with coworkers at work, such as the experiences recounted in this chapter, are among the most exciting, rewarding missionary experiences of my life. These are some of the principles that I have extracted from these experiences.

First, there are many people at work who believe in God and are anxious to talk about Him.

Second, explaining what we believe is not the only way to

---

*Henry J. Eyring, *Mormon Scientist* (2007), 4.

explicitly share the gospel. We can *use* what we believe to help others understand and solve important problems. The model of testifying at work can be different from the model we use at Church: We simply need to *use* the gospel. In fact, this is one way in which the Savior invited us to bear testimony: "If any man will do his will, he shall know of the doctrine, whether it be of God, or whether I speak of myself" (John 7:17).

Third, because the truth works, there is no reason why we ever need to feel timid in using it. The gospel is extraordinarily flexible because truth is broadly applicable. We are able to draw upon the truths of the gospel to help resolve very different types of problems. Just as we have been taught to put footnotes in essays when we use an idea from another person, we should simply be sure that our coworkers understand where the principles came from as we use the gospel to solve problems.

Fourth, we should describe gospel principles in the same matter-of-fact tone of voice with which we might draw upon an article in the *Wall Street Journal* or *Science.* Insight is insight, and truth is truth. There is no need to keep the language of religion segregated from the language of business, science, or academia. When we have a common language, our friends and colleagues at work can teach us things about religion, and vice versa.

And finally, fifth: Just as we can in our testimony meetings, our friends at work can feel the Spirit of God as we *use* the gospel. President Hugh B. Brown summarized these observations this way: "We don't need to 'defend' the gospel in a military sense. Rather, we should do with religion as we do with music, not defend it but simply *render it.* It needs no defense."*

The Memories of Hugh B. Brown: An Abundant Life, Edwin B. Firmage, ed. (1988), 136.

CHAPTER 5

Set Goals and Deadlines
to Guide Your Work

Some people are so well organized that they finish their home teaching before the tenth of every month. I, ashamedly, am a procrastinator. I do it at the end of every month. And thank goodness someone announced that it needed to be done by the end of every month, because without that deadline, I would keep putting it off until next week. I need a deadline.

I suspect, however, that those who get home teaching done by the tenth of every month also need to set deadlines in order to get things done. They just set a deadline earlier in the month.

My gas, phone, water, and electric companies, as well as my credit card companies and the Internal Revenue Service, also impose deadlines monthly, quarterly, or annually to be sure that I pay my bills. If they didn't, I would probably keep forgetting to pay them. Goals and deadlines, in other words, help almost all of us do what we need to do.

In contrast to home teaching, which has used the last day of the month as a *de facto* deadline, the member missionary effort has never imposed deadlines. As a result, most of us are not engaged in finding people for the missionaries to teach. Most of us want to be good missionaries—and we intend to start next week.

In 1984, Elder M. Russell Ballard challenged us in general conference to periodically set a date as a goal or deadline by which we would find someone to bring into our homes for the missionaries to teach. He promised us that if we would pick a date and not a person, and then do everything we could to discuss the gospel with as many people as possible, that the Lord would bless us to be able to find someone by that date who would accept our invitation to study the gospel with the missionaries.* For some reason this talk had a powerful impact on me—probably because I was a ward mission leader. I got a strong feeling that this challenge was something that I specifically needed to do.

In my prayers that evening I set a date, conveniently about a year away, as part of this covenant with the Lord. I then committed that I would do all I could to engage in gospel discussions with as many different people as possible, and I restated to the Lord what I understood to be Elder Ballard's promise. The first people I found for the missionaries to teach were the Singleton family (Tom was my basketball friend). The next year I set a date again and was able to introduce a coworker and his wife to the missionaries.

In each of the subsequent years I have set a date in this manner, and in each instance God has blessed me to find someone whom I could introduce to the missionaries. Most have not joined the Church. In almost every instance, I could not have predicted who was going to accept the invitation. But I have learned that I can predict with absolute certainty that I will find *someone*.

Can everyone do this successfully? Yes—but there actually is a method to it, which (I hope) emerges from the stories that follow.

---

*See M. Russell Ballard, "Write Down a Date," *Ensign*, November 1984.

On the Plane to Hawaii

I had set a date of January 31, 1993. In typical fashion, early January had come and I had asked a number of people but had failed to find anyone who evidenced interest. I was scheduled to travel to Honolulu for an academic conference on January 20. The way my schedule looked for the rest of the month, it seemed clear that I had to meet the person I could introduce to the missionaries on my flights to or from Honolulu. There was just no other time to do it. So I prayed that God would cause a person who would accept my invitation to hear the missionary discussions to sit next to me on that plane to Hawaii.

After all that fervent effort and prayer, I just couldn't believe the person who sat next to me on that flight. Instead of someone who would be interested in a discussion about religion, my seatmate was a thirty-three-year-old man wearing shorts and a loud Hawaiian shirt that was open to his sternum, with thick, curly chest hair billowing out and three gold chains around his neck. I tried to strike up a conversation. He told me that he was a stonemason from Hartford who worked eleven months every year to save enough to escape to Hawaii for a month in the winter to chase women. He then proceeded to tell me how much he enjoyed seeing four particularly beautiful women every year when he returned to Honolulu. I was *so* disappointed. I had tried so hard and prayed so hard to find someone, and instead I got stuck next to a playboy who didn't have a religious bone in his body. Discouraged, I politely wished him a good time and turned to some reading I had brought with me. He rented headphones and proceeded to flip his fingers to the rhythm of the rock-and-roll tunes that blasted out his ears.

When the flight attendant brought lunch around, I had to put my reading away, and I started a small-talk conversation with my seatmate. He asked if I had ever been to Hawaii before, and I responded that I had, to attend a two-month language training school en route to a mission I had served for the Mormon church in Korea twenty years ago. The man then put his fork down, looked at me, and said, "So you're a Mormon?" I responded that I was, and he said, "You know, the funniest thing has been happening to me over the past year or so. I have just had this growing curiosity to know more about Mormons. I don't know why. Could you tell me a little about your church?"

Could I? I then felt something like a cocoon descend and envelop us, and for the next three hours we discussed the gospel of Jesus Christ. There was a wonderful spirit there. Eventually we began speaking of other things, and I ultimately excused myself to finish some writing I needed to do. Several times during the remainder of the flight, however, he interrupted me to say thanks for telling him about my church. At his final interruption, I told him that we had missionaries in Hartford, and I was sure that they would be willing to visit him when he returned home, to explain our beliefs in more depth. He asked if instead there might not be missionaries in Honolulu, so I took his address and promised to have them visit him.

Ted Blackstone

During one summer vacation to Utah, we had a chance to attend the open house for the Mount Timpanogos Temple. It was a silent walking tour, and the experience troubled me. Our Boston Temple recently had been announced, and I could see us walking through it at the time of our open house with friends, unable to say or explain anything as we walked through the dressing rooms, baptistry, and celestial and sealing rooms. I realized that if taking my acquaintances to our open house was my way of introducing them to the Church, it would likely just be to them an interesting view of Mormon temple architecture. I resolved at that time that I would set a date early enough in the year 2000 that I could have gone through the missionary discussions with someone *before* the open house. That way the open house would be the culmination of a learning experience, rather than an introduction to one. I therefore set my date as June 30, 2000—two months before the open house was scheduled to begin.

However, as usual, I postponed things for several months and then started desperately inviting all sorts of unlikely people to take the missionary discussions. Then one day in mid-June a former student, Ted Blackstone, visited me, and as he sat on the couch in my office I just had this sense that I should invite Ted to take the missionary discussions. He knew a bit about my faith, though I knew almost nothing of his and had not thought before that he might be someone I could invite. To my surprise, he accepted, and we began the discussions, which were led by a masterful missionary, Jared Sine, and his companions.

Little by little, as we progressed through the discussions, Ted became more serious. After a particularly poignant fifth discussion in mid-August, in which I lost my composure inviting him to be baptized, I said, "You know, Ted, if you keep waiting to be baptized until you know for sure that this is the true gospel of Jesus Christ, you may wait for a very long time." I then read him the verse from the gospel of John that asserts, "If any man will do his will, he shall know of the doctrine, whether it be of God, or whether I speak of myself" (John 7:17). I told Ted that one of the surest ways he could know of the truth was to commit to be baptized, because this act of doing God's will was the way he could know of its truth. I further asserted that while he could attend the upcoming open house for the temple in September in any event, if he was baptized he could then attend the temple's dedication as a member of the Church. I suggested September 9.

We agreed to fast together the next Sunday to help Ted reach his decision. The next evening Ted called. He said that his aunt, who lived in Phoenix and had converted to the Church many years earlier, had called him saying that she had this feeling that something big was going on in Ted's life, and she wanted to be able to help him. That helped Ted feel that God really did have a personal interest in this decision, and he called me to say that he was going to be baptized. The baptismal service and his subsequent confirmation and ordination were wonderful experiences. On the Sunday he was confirmed, Ted asked Bishop Ott if he could bear his testimony. He said that he had come to realize that baptism was an act of faith, not a step taken based upon sure knowledge.

Friends subsequently arranged for Ted to have a ticket to be in the celestial room of the temple during its dedication. As President Gordon B. Hinckley was offering his dedicatory prayer, Ted felt a rushing wind come into the room and enter his body, changing his heart forever.

Our family had a wonderful experience too, as our seats in the dedication were in the small preparation room attached to the men's dressing room. Fortunately for us, the Singleton family was there, allowing me to reflect on those wonderful, often tearful testimonies I was able to bear to them as we had participated in teaching them the discussions years earlier. I just couldn't have felt more blessed.

Natasha Paton

In 2001 I set three dates, and for the first two had found someone who had decided not to continue with the missionaries after we had finished the first discussion. In my work with ward mission leaders as a counselor in the Massachusetts Boston Mission presidency, I repeatedly asserted, "You cannot be a successful ward mission leader if you cannot speak of sharing the gospel using present-tense verbs and first-person pronouns." Hence, I had created a bit of pressure for myself.

So in early summer I set another date, October 15, and then followed the usual practice of postponing action. In late August I told the elders serving in our ward of my date, asking for their prayers, and I began looking actively for opportunities to invite people. My tactic had become to always plant within my conversations terms that associated me with Mormonism, as noted previously. True to form, I had not been able to find anyone who expressed any interest. I then began to panic, causing me to invite all sorts of improbable people to take the discussions. But one by one the possibilities seemed to exhaust themselves.

By the end of September I had resigned myself to failing this time. It was the busiest semester in my life, and I simply could see no way that I was going to be able to meet anyone new by my date of October 15. I decided that I would just drop the date this time because I felt that the Lord knew I was doing all that I could to serve in His kingdom. I thought that it would be okay, just this once when I was so extraordinarily busy, to let other people be the member missionaries. After a few days in this mind-set, however, I decided I had better not succumb to that rationale because if I did, I would systematically opt out of this assignment in the future because I would always be too busy. I therefore recommitted to God that I would do all I could to find someone. But I began shifting the focus of my prayers, asking God to send someone *to me* who wanted to know about the Church. I promised that I would invite him or her when I saw that person.

On October 12, Christine and I spoke to the Latter-day Saint Student Association group from the Harvard Business School in the Cambridge chapel, summarizing important insights we had taken from our work in researching and writing a history of the Church in the Boston area. A few of the students had brought friends of other faiths, and there was a warm, sweet spirit in the meeting. At the end, as we mingled with the students, one of my own students, Natasha Paton, came up to me and asked, "Professor Christensen, I understand there is a set of lessons about your church for people who want to know about it. Is there any way that I could take those in your home?" I stood there stunned; it was all I could do not to cry. Natasha had no idea how her action represented such a direct answer to my efforts and my prayers. We subsequently held the discussions with Natasha and her husband, Andrew (who had been a less-active member, unbeknownst to me), in our home, and, as always, they were sweet spiritual experiences. Natasha was baptized on June 8, 2002. She and Andrew were sealed in the Boston Temple a year later.

Howard Littlefield

A few years after our experience with Natasha, I had set a deadline of August 31. About two months before the date, I turned up the heat and asked *a lot* of people over the next weeks if they might be willing to come to our home to meet the missionaries. Truly, nobody—and I mean nobody—was interested. I faced the very real possibility that for the first time in twenty-two years, I might not find someone by my date. But on August 29 I was driving to Stamford, Connecticut, with a new British doctoral student, Howard Littlefield, who had volunteered to help me write a case. As we drove, I mentioned my membership in our church, and Howard's eyes lit up. He said he had been very active in the Anglican Church but had been quite disappointed that the Episcopal Church near Harvard Square was shut down for the summer. I told him about our singles wards that met in the Longfellow Park chapel and asked if he'd be interested in going to their meetings until the Episcopalians geared up for the school year. He readily accepted. I then suggested that he might benefit from coming to our home to meet with our missionaries, just so he would know what to expect, and he accepted that invitation, too.

That evening over dinner I told my family that I had found Howard for the missionaries to teach, but then groused, "Why can't I find the person weeks or months before the date? Why does the Lord have to string me out to the very last minute?"

My son Spencer replied, "Dad, I've seen this happen often enough that I think I know what's going on. Several months before your date you're so relaxed about it that the Lord can't trust you. If He puts someone in your path, He doesn't know if He can trust you to invite that person. But two things happen. First, you take seriously your commitment to find someone. And second, as the date approaches, you become more and more desperate. And when you become desperate, the Lord can trust you. He knows that you'll invite anybody He puts into your path."

I labeled this phenomenon "Spencer's Principle of Desperation."

～

Every time I have set a date—first to invite someone, and then to find someone who says yes, God has blessed me to intersect with someone who has accepted my invitation to come into our home to study with the missionaries. I have noted above only a few of the experiences from which I learned important lessons. Most of these people, of course, did not accept baptism—and that's fine. I succeed when I invite. And in almost every case, we have emerged from the experience with a stronger friendship with the people we invited into our home. Also, again in every case, there is no way I could have predicted in advance who would accept or reject my invitations.

Out of these experiences in setting dates, I have learned a few important lessons. First, Spencer's Principle of Desperation is a general principle. When we engage in a covenant with God that we will do something that one of our leaders has asked us to do, and we are desperate to do what we have committed to do, God truly comes to trust us. He came to trust Abraham (see Genesis 18:17–19); and He can come to trust you and me. I think that a reason why so many people have set a date but then never found someone for the missionaries to teach is that they never became desperate. The date was a casual commitment.

The second insight is that setting a date is not a program. Making commitments to God is a principle of obedience and improvement that can and should bless every dimension of our lives. I wonder if a key reason why the missionary work sometimes flounders is that too few members take seriously the commitment we made when we were baptized "to stand as witnesses of God at all times and in all things, and in all places" (Mosiah 18:9).

And third: I think that as we get busy in our family, church, and secular lives, our inclination when confronted with uncomfortable commandments or instructions from Church leaders is to rationalize—to assert that because we are already stretched to the limit, we are doing enough, and our particular extenuating circumstances exempt us from having to obey those specific words of counsel or commandment. These experiences have taught me that the busier we get, the more important it becomes, actually, that we exercise the childlike faith of Nephi: "I will go and do the things which the Lord hath commanded, for I know that the Lord giveth no commandments unto the children of men, save he shall prepare a way for them that they may accomplish the thing which he commandeth them" (1 Nephi 3:7).

In the equation that determines whether we can find people for the missionaries to teach, God's role is a constant, not a variable. He always keeps His promises. The only variable is whether we have the faith that we will be blessed with miracles if we make commitments to God and then obediently do what we said we would do.

CHAPTER 6

Questions and Answers on the Internet

We have seen two Webs in the past fifteen years. The first was unidirectional, often called Web 1.0, in which people who were looking for information could find, read, and download it. We are now surrounded by Web 2.0, which is a multidirectional, conversational Web. In it we can communicate, ask questions, and receive answers through search engines and websites, Facebook and other social media pages and groups, and through verbal and written conversations, blogs, speeches, debates, messaging, and tweeting.

Opponents to the Church have established websites that bombard people who seek information about the Church with false or misguided information instead. Indeed, a study in 2005 by the More Good Foundation discovered that if someone typed in common phrases or words about the Church—words like "Mormon missionaries," "Mormon temples," "Mormon history," and so on—between 80 and 90 percent of the websites search engines identified were antagonistic to the Church.

In response, starting in 2005 the More Good Foundation and other initiatives by Church members have launched many websites whose URLs refer to LDS or Mormon names. They continue to work to populate these sites with positive content. Simultaneously, the Church has transformed LDS.org and Mormon.org into Web 2.0 sites that are among the best religious sites on the Internet, where people with questions find it easy to find clear answers. Our leaders have urged us to post our personal testimonies on these sites—but while posting our profiles and testimonies on good websites is important, these are discrete events. We have wanted to learn how sharing the gospel on the Web can become a way of life for us. In the following pages I'll summarize some hypotheses that we are formulating about how to share the gospel online. We have much to learn—but we're sharing these ideas in preliminary form in the hope that they will help you, and so that you can help us.

USING THE INTERNET AS A TOOL FOR MISSIONARY WORK

In a Young Single Adult conference in Boston in October 2009, Elder M. Russell Ballard of the Quorum of the Twelve Apostles spoke about the need to begin sharing the gospel online. In response, we established a "digital mission" through which we could learn how to do this.

About twenty-five members were called as stake digital missionaries, led by Teppo Jouttenus, Natalie Williams, and Reed Davis. Three others—Emily Tanner, Melanie Ensign, and Brigham Frandsen—were called as zone leaders. At the beginning we had thought that reversing Satan's land-grab of Web 1.0 meant writing and posting positive essays that people who were looking for answers could download. It was a one-directional concept—from us to them, without a way to have a conversation. In contrast, blogs are tools to create conversations about how to use the gospel to solve problems. Each zone decided that building a blog, rather than dispensing answers, would create more opportunities to find people who have questions—the key for missionary work. Their blogs are named MormonPerspectives.com, NextDoorMormon.com, and RealLifeAnswers.org. Each focused on a different dimension of what it feels like to be a member of the Church. In their first year, each attracted nearly 40,000 unique visitors.

The digital missionaries are asked to serve between five to eight hours per week. About half of their time is to be spent on their roles for their blog. The other half is to be spent finding people who have questions about the LDS Church or about religious issues in general and are looking for answers on the Internet. Our digital missionaries offer to help them find the answers they need.

After keeping our stake digital mission small and focused for the first year to learn how to lead this effort, we have now asked the ward mission leaders in each ward to suggest that the bishop call one or two ward members as ward digital missionaries. We are assigning them to serve online as members of one of the three zones. In turn, these ward missionaries invite other members of their wards who have other callings to be "guest bloggers." This way, sharing the gospel on the Internet isn't a program, an event, or a calling given to a few. Rather, we hope that eventually this can become a way of life for all members, week after week.

In building their blogs, two or three of the digital missionaries in each zone became the *main writers*—the ones who defined and evolved the intellectual issues that the blog is addressing. We call the other missionaries in the zone *reactors:* They read the main blog contributions and then comment on or extend their basic ideas. *Extenders* are the third group. They spend their time connecting the blog with people they know who might be interested in the ideas in the blog. Because the number and type of connections between the blog and other websites and blogs determines the ranking the blog achieves, the work of all three roles that the missionaries play has proven to be critical. They have worked together to help people who have questions about the Church find people who can converse with them on questions that are important.

We sense that there is a broad need to discuss religious topics online—and that the need is far from being satiated. For example, the following table lists a sample of religious questions people were asking on the Internet during a month in early 2012. The left-hand column lists words or phrases that are entered in Google. They represent underlying issues and concerns that people want to learn about. The second and third columns show the number of people in the world and in the United States who searched the Internet to find information and opinion on these topics in a typical month (in millions of people).

Phrase Searched	Global Searches	U.S. Searches
What is love	226	45.5
What is death	83.1	30.2
Family	83.1	37.2
God	55.6	16.6
Sin	45.5	4.1
Marriage	24.9	9.1
Hope	13.6	6.1
Prayer	13.6	4.1
Genealogy	5.0	1.5
Happiness	5.0	1.5
Temptation	2.2	0.5
Forgiveness	1.0	0.7

Look, for example, at the first line. In the month in which we retrieved the data, this shows that 226 million people in the world, including 45.5 million people in the United States, typed in the phrase "What is love" to guide Google as it searched the web for articles, news, and blogs on this topic. That's right. Two hundred twenty-six *million* people in a month. Google ranks each of these topics as "low," meaning that this topic isn't overly crowded yet—and a blog could attract a significant following.

When Mara and Danny Kofoed decided to begin sharing the gospel online in 2011, they created a blog called ablogaboutlove .com to attract some of those millions of people who were interested in the topic, "What is love?" If you can, please put this book down and visit their website now. (Danny was in our stake, but he married Mara and they defected to Brooklyn, unfortunately.) Their blog focuses on love and everyday struggles we face in life. They received well over a million unique hits in their first nine months. Their approach to missionary work is to focus on being open and honest with the things they struggle with. Their goal is to help others who are going through similar things or just need somebody to talk to. They do not push their religion on anybody but are very open about what they believe, and, if asked about it, they will share their beliefs and testimony. They also developed a way to take their online conversations and meet people in person. Such an approach is not appropriate for all individuals, but it could be adapted into your own online efforts.

As another option, you might focus your blog on a less popular or local topic that might be less crowded with other blogs. A sample of this comes from MormonPerspectives.com. In 2011, a digital missionary wrote a review on the *Book of Mormon Musical.* This post went viral and quickly appeared in the top five Google results for the phrase "Book of Mormon Musical," and it still appears there today. This singular post reaches thousands each month.

In my own efforts to share the gospel online as best I can, sometimes I have written essays for one of our blogs. Other times, I'll pen an essay and post it to my personal website. One of the essays is my testimony. I titled it, "Why I Belong, and Why I Believe"; I originally wrote it for my children on my fiftieth birthday. I subsequently posted it to my website (claytonchristensen .com), where visitors can easily see it. Here are portions of one response I received from a woman I have never met who somehow had come upon my testimony:

"I have just read through your love letter to your children (twice). It is a beautiful testament. I am moved—and more curious than I would have expected. I hear very disturbing things about the Mormon faith and its history with people of color. However, . . . one of my mother's dear friends was a Mormon. She was wonderful. Once she took my brother and me to a service—I'll never forget the feeling of love and welcome we felt. Every Mormon I've met has been loving and kind, caring and committed. This topic has always been a source of cognitive dissonance for me. I will do a bit of research on the Mormon religion. I want to know more."

I cannot describe my feelings of gratitude that through the Web I could meet someone of her stature. I truly am excited that I have a new friend—and look forward to building a friendship upon testimony and the Spirit. Our online missionaries and I have wonderful experiences like this many times every month. It is a great way to share the gospel.

I mentioned in the introduction to this book that when I called myself on a mission again, the Spirit of God returned in my life. I invite you to do this. I invite you not because it is easy. It is hard. But it is worth it.

What We Have Learned as We've Shared the Gospel Online

We have learned a number of important points (so far) about online missionary work. The first is personal conversion. When the online missionaries and guest bloggers from the ward (of which there can be as many as we can handle to help follow up with) are given the assignment to write a post, it is much like being asked to speak in sacrament meeting or prepare a lesson. There is a direction to scripture study. There is a deadline and an urgency. As the online missionaries and guest bloggers have taken the time to personally study, ponder, and formulate their thoughts and feelings, *their* testimonies have deepened. Personal conversion and thus confidence for sharing the gospel face-to-face have been greatly enhanced by the missionaries' and guests' work online. They have been able to articulate these testimonies. Online they refine and reformulate their statements before they touch "send."

We have a growing sense that this is particularly true among members of the church age fourteen through twenty-five. Most of them are online anyway, and if we don't call them to serve as online missionaries, they will find other things to do online. In many ways, the call to be online missionaries is a calling to share the gospel in their native tongue.

We realized only a handful of youth during their teenage years have regular opportunities to share their testimonies with nonmembers. We felt that asking them to serve as digital missionaries was a perfect way to help them have regular missionary opportunities and also help them learn how to better articulate their beliefs. To test this theory, we called Jackson Haight, a high school sophomore, to be a digital missionary. He was mentored closely by the digital mission leadership and started to write posts for one of the blogs. He said it was hard in the beginning because he had never had to put his testimony into words that would be viewed by thousands. He also knew he had to make sure he wasn't sharing false doctrine. He spent hours reading the scriptures and the words of the living prophets to make sure his own words were correct. He worked hard to express his beliefs in concise writing that could be understood by a wide audience. One of his posts, for example, was shared more than seven hundred times through social media and viewed by thousands.

Through this process, Jackson found that the messages of his posts began to flow more easily into his everyday conversations with friends. His confidence in sharing the gospel grew. In September 2012, he baptized and later conferred the Aaronic Priesthood upon his good friend Keith and ordained him to the office of a priest. In October 2012, we developed a fourth blog named YoungAndMormon.com. This blog is now being run under the direction of the stake Young Men and Young Women presidencies and the digital mission team. When Jackson shared his experience with the stake youth council, the Spirit was powerful as he explained how he had been pondering the word for himself. Other members of the council have since been called as digital missionaries and have committed to participate regularly on the blog. Jackson Haight has truly been an example of the scripture "Whosoever shall lose his life for my sake and the gospel's, the same shall save it" (Mark 8:35). When Jackson is called on a full-time mission, he truly will be fluent in online and personal languages.

Second, our online missionaries have found it quite easy to invite friends who are not yet active members of the Church to serve with them—asking them to contribute to their blogs as they serve. Often this entails sending to nonmember friends a draft of what they have written, asking for feedback before they post it to their blog. Their friends invariably are very helpful, and, of course, this gives the digital missionaries ways to share the gospel with their friends in ways that otherwise would not be easy. This has been so effective for the quality of writing *and* for sharing the gospel that we have, in fact, made this a sort of requirement before posting. We could fill a book of stories about how sharing the gospel via blogging creates many opportunities to ask friends to help us (as described in chapter 3).

Third, I have noted several times that because we can't predict in advance who will and will not be interested in the gospel, the more people we meet, the more we can invite, and the more people we will find for the missionaries to teach. I am fortunate because at work I meet a lot of new people. Others of us, however, find themselves in personal and professional situations in which they have few opportunities to meet new people. Many faithful full-time mothers with young children at home find it hard to meet new friends by the very nature of their profession, for example. Whether they live in Orem, Odessa, or Orlando, most of their friends are members of the Church—and this makes it quite hard to do missionary work. The opportunity to serve as online missionaries and guest bloggers gives them many more avenues to meet new people. A friend who has built an active blog reminded me that the missionaries need to knock on door after door, in a trial-and-error way, in order to find people who will talk about the Church. In contrast, those who are sharing the gospel online are able to see more clearly who is interested and who isn't, simply by studying the questions that people are asking.

Fourth, we concluded that working alone can be discouraging and draining at times. Online missionaries need to feel a part of a team, and it worked well for us to organize the digital mission by zones. Our zone leaders tried to hold zone conferences monthly in which they could train one another, share inspiring experiences, solve common problems, and follow up with the "deadlines" of posts written by the missionaries and the ever-growing group of guest bloggers.

And finally, this: As a signal travels over longer and longer distances on a wire, its power attenuates or diminishes and its clarity gets garbled by static. In contrast, the clarity and the power of the Spirit of God does not diminish by distance—even if your new friends live on the other side of the world. If you write online through the power of the Spirit and love of the Lord, the new friends that you'll meet will be able to feel that Spirit and that love—as if they were speaking with you face-to-face. Of this I testify.

We invite you to visit frequently our website

everydaymissionaries.org

as you read this book. Tell other readers what you learn as you follow the principles for sharing the gospel—and tell your stories that will inspire the rest of us!

PART 2

TEACHING TOWARD CONVERSION

Many of us misdiagnose the reason why so many investigators don't follow through on their commitments to read and ponder the Book of Mormon, to pray to learn if it is true, and to attend church. When investigators repeatedly fail to keep these commitments, we and the missionaries are prone to conclude that the investigators really are not interested. But often investigators don't do these things because they don't know how. Many are articulate. But in their churches and homes, prayers were memorized, not expressed from the heart.

Yes, they can read. But they learned to read novels and textbooks, where you began at the beginning and ended at the end. Scriptures, by contrast, often should be read to answer questions.*

Surprisingly, few investigators know how to keep the Sabbath day holy. They've never done it before. Neither do they know how to get the most out of church attendance.

---

*See *Preach My Gospel,* 107–12.

Because most investigators don't know how to read the scriptures, pray to God, and keep the Sabbath holy, the vast majority of new investigators do not progress to baptism. When we take the time to teach them how to do these things, many more are baptized. Helping others learn how to do these things is the focus of part 2 of this book. As before, I will use true stories as parables and close by summarizing what we might glean from them.

CHAPTER 7

Teach How to Pray

Several years ago we invited Joshua Moore and his wife, Angela (who was a less-active member), to come to our home to meet with the missionaries. Joshua had been raised in a Christian home but had never attended any church regularly. Joshua had a first-rate education and was a venture capitalist in Boston. They were expecting their first baby.

Elders Murphy and Adams, who were laboring in our ward at that time, were great teachers. Our mission president had been emphasizing how important it was to keep lesson appointments to no longer than forty-five minutes, the optimal time recommended in *Preach My Gospel*. In the first lesson Joshua had lots of questions, and it took the full forty-five minutes to deliver the material that the elders felt needed to be delivered. So at the end of the lesson they gave Joshua a copy of the Book of Mormon and invited him to read and pray about it. Joshua said that he would.

At the beginning of the second lesson Elder Adams asked Joshua if he had read any of the Book of Mormon and if he had been praying. When he said yes, the elders seemed pleased and

93

quickly got down to the business of teaching Joshua and Angela the second lesson. The lesson took longer than planned. Glancing at his watch, Elder Murphy saw that the discussion was bumping up against the forty-five-minute mark, and he finished his last point as quickly as he could. Following my wife's closing prayer, Elder Adams asked Joshua if he would continue reading the Book of Mormon and praying every day. Joshua said he would.

The third lesson was a repeat of the second. Elder Adams began by asking Joshua if he had been reading the Book of Mormon and praying. When Joshua said he had, the elders complimented him and asked if he had any questions. Joshua said that he had none, and the elders then began teaching their carefully prepared lesson. Again, with so much to explain, the lesson ran to the end of the allotted time. As they closed, Elder Adams reiterated, "Will you continue to read and pray, Joshua?" He again promised that he would, and after making an appointment for the next lesson, the elders left.

At the beginning of the fourth lesson, it was clear that the light of the gospel that one normally sees in the faces of those who are discovering the truth just wasn't radiating from Joshua's. So when he told the elders again that he had been studying and praying, I decided to probe more deeply by asking, "Joshua, how are you praying, and what are you saying in your prayers?"

Looking sheepish but relieved, Joshua answered, "I guess I really don't know how to pray. I was raised in a Christian home, but I never really learned how to pray. I learned a few set prayers when I was a boy, but I can't remember them now. I've been telling you that I've been praying because I was too embarrassed to admit that I don't know how. I actually have never thought about prayer, one way or another."

I apologized for not helping Joshua with this, and the

missionaries set aside the teaching plan they had prepared. I of-fered, "You've heard us pray at the beginning and end of our dis-cussions together, Joshua, but these are public prayers where we say things that pertain to all of us. Your personal prayers should be different; they're more like a personal report or conversation with God. Let's kneel, and I'll demonstrate how I would pray if I were in your shoes. Then I'll ask Christine to pray, and then Elder Murphy. Listen to what we say and how we say it. Each of the prayers will be different, but listen for patterns in what we say. Then let's sit in our chairs and you can ask us any questions about prayer that you'd like."

After we had done this, I asked, "What patterns did you see in the way we prayed?"

"Well, the most obvious thing is that you all prayed aloud, in-stead of just thinking the prayer in your mind. Do you always pray aloud when you're praying in private?"

"Silent prayers are okay," Elder Murphy responded. "But whenever you can, pray aloud. The reason is that it helps you feel like you're really speaking to God—because that's what you're do-ing, having a personal conversation with our Father in Heaven."

Joshua then said, "Each of you began your prayer by thanking God for things He has given us. I'm assuming that this helps us realize how much God loves us. Right?"

When Elder Adams agreed, Joshua then asked, "I noticed that you didn't just ask for blessings, but you *explained* things to Him—told Him what you had done and what you were planning to do, and *then* asked for His guidance. Why did you do that?"

Elder Adams answered, "Think of it this way. When your chil-dren talk to you by phone, you want to hear their report on what they've been doing. You have a pretty good idea of what they're up to, but you love them so much that you just want to hear them tell about themselves. Right? Well, God wants to hear from us because He really does love us. He *wants* us to think things through in our own minds and make our own decisions about what would be the right thing to do. Then we ask for His opinion of our decisions. He wants it this way because if He made all the decisions for us, we would never grow. That's how I visualize personal prayer; it's like calling home to my parents. And it's clear from the scriptures that Heavenly Father *wants* us to 'call home' because He loves us, wants to hear our voices, and wants to give us His advice."

The discussion seemed to pique Joshua's curiosity about prayer. He asked, "When I talk things over with God and ask for His help, what sorts of topics can I raise? For example, do you ask God only for help with spiritual things, or can you pray about problems at work?"

Elder Murphy asked Joshua to read Alma 34:17–27. When he had finished, Joshua summarized what he had learned. "I guess what this says is that anything that is important to me is important to God. Am I right?"

"That's really true, Joshua," Elder Murphy taught. "It is overwhelming to think that God, who has so much power and wisdom, loves us so much that anything that is important to us is important to Him." He then asked Joshua if he would kneel with them again and pray verbally in the way they had just discussed. Joshua offered a beautiful, heartfelt prayer.

Joshua then asked, "So far you've taught me how to talk to God. How does He talk to me?"

I then took the license to say, "This is my way to frame it. We speak to each other in physical, analog ways. Our vocal chords vibrate. This initiates waves in the air, which are also physical. These waves hit the eardrums of others, causing them to vibrate, which in turn creates tiny electrical signals that transport those vibrating patterns to the listeners' brains. In turn, the signals initiate neurons to zip around our brains, distilling the concept that the speaker wanted to convey. The key concept is that these are physical, mechanical phenomena. We don't hear with our ears, we hear with our brains. Our wonderful ears are converters; they transform mechanical into electronic signals.

"So far as we know, these physical, mechanical waves that convey speech don't work in space, where there is no atmosphere. So if two astronauts took off their helmets on the moon and tried to talk to each other, it wouldn't work, because there is no air in which vibrations can be converted into waves. So they need to talk electronically, not mechanically.

"This is a long way of saying that you should not expect God to speak to you by these physical waves that your ears collect. Rather, He dispatches the Holy Ghost, which is the Spirit of God, to you, and His spirit can communicate to *your* spirit inside of you directly to your brain or your feelings—without going through mechanical-electrical conversions in your ears. A lot of people get confused because they try to hear God's voice with their ears, and they don't hear anything. Instead, you need to listen *inside* of yourself. Sometimes you detect His voice as ideas, words, or sentences that just emerge inside of your head as thoughts. More often, you detect His message as a peaceful, warm feeling inside your heart. It is as if the Spirit of God went inside of you and gave your spirit a warm hug to say that 'This is right.'"

When we had finished, Elder Adams asked, "Joshua and Angela, we'd like you to do two things every day. First, will you each find a quiet time each day, when you are alone, and pray out loud to our Heavenly Father in the way you have just done? And before you go to bed, will you kneel together and pray as husband and wife about the things that concern your marriage and your family? Will you do these things?" Joshua and Angela agreed that they would.

Elder Murphy asked Joshua's permission to call in a couple of days to be sure it was going as hoped. Joshua said he would welcome the call. The elders did make that call, and Joshua responded with some pride in his voice that he and Angela had indeed been praying as they had said they would. When they met for their next meeting, the glow that I had not seen in Joshua's face before was finally there. He was baptized a short time later.

Joshua and Angela have been sealed in the temple and now have four wonderful children. I shudder to think that, had we not discovered his inability to pray, the missionaries would likely have put him on the "not progressing" list of former investigators.

When we see investigators not following through on the commitments they have made to pray, read, and attend church, it may well be because they don't know how to do those things. Even if they have degrees from the best universities (like Joshua), we should not assume that they know how to communicate with God, or (as we'll see next) how to study the word of God. Our default assumption should be that they don't know how.

CHAPTER 8

Teach How to Study the Book of Mormon Prayerfully

Our experience with Joshua and Angela Moore and the experiences I will recount in this chapter have profoundly changed the way that we lead our friends toward conversion. In addition to teaching them how to pray, we need to teach people *how* to read and ponder the scriptures—specifically, how to engage in private, prayerful study of the Book of Mormon. This became clear to me through some experiences with a business associate I had known for several years, Brian Carpenter. Brian sent me an e-mail in which he expressed curiosity about our church's views on several issues, and I invited him to our home to discuss these with the missionaries over dinner. In extending the invitation, I said, "Rather than our telling you what we want you to know about our church, could you please come with a list of questions about religion that you've not been able to find satisfactory answers to? Then we can give our views on those issues. We just want to be sure we're responsive to what's on your mind."

Brian came on a Thursday evening with a typed list of very thoughtful questions in which he puzzled about the concepts of

99

original sin and infant baptism, among others. We talked about these over dinner to be sure we understood why these were important to him and how he had tried to find answers. We then adjourned to our living room and asked the missionaries to answer several of the questions at the top of his list. They skillfully drew upon the four lessons in chapter 3 of *Preach My Gospel* to do so. They then described the Book of Mormon, testified that it contained answers to all of Brian's questions, handed him a copy, and asked if he would read it. Brian was highly educated and had been raised in a Christian home, but he pushed the book away, saying, "Somebody gave me one of these several years ago. I tried to read it into "Second Neffee," but it's weird and I just couldn't get into it."

As Brian said those words, I felt a strong impression that possibly the reason why the Book of Mormon loomed as such a chore to Brian was that, although he was certainly literate and had attended other churches, he might never have learned *how* to read the scriptures.

So I said, "Brian, when we read novels and textbooks in school, we learned to begin at the beginning and end at the end. But that's not always the most effective way to read the scriptures. To help you learn to read in a different way, I'm going to give you a homework assignment. You'll need to turn it in when we meet next week. I'm going to write it down. This will take you about two hours to complete, so you should block off time to do this on some evening or next Sunday. It should be quiet time where you can be alone and not be interrupted."

The assignment I gave Brian was this: Read just two chapters in the Book of Mormon: Mosiah 18:1–16 and Moroni 8. Then write a two-paragraph answer to each of these three questions:

- Why does it make God so angry when people baptize little children?

- Why does God want us to be baptized in the first place? What is the purpose of baptism?

- What is the process by which we come to be forgiven of our sins?

I picked these because questions about the doctrines of infant baptism and original sin were on the list Brian had brought, and the answers are included in these chapters. I then described the process Brian needed to follow when doing this "homework." It entailed seven steps, so I wrote it down underneath the questions:

1. Pray, on your knees, aloud, telling God that you got this homework assignment from your friend. Ask Him to help you understand the chapters as you read them.

2. Read the chapters.

3. Write your answers, in draft form, to the three questions.

4. Kneel again in verbal prayer and explain to God the answers you have written, just as if you were talking to Him face-to-face. Then tell Him you're going to read the chapters one more time. Ask Him again to please help you understand even more deeply the answers that *He* would want you to give to these questions as you read.

5. Read the chapters again.

6. Revise your answers, based upon your deeper understanding. These written answers are the "homework" you need to give us when we meet next.

7. Then kneel again and pray a third time. But the purpose of this prayer will be different. This time you need to ask God if the things that you have written, and the things that you have read, are true.

After reviewing the assignment to be sure Brian understood it, we read Moroni 10:3–5 and said, "Now we want to teach you how to give that prayer in step 7." We pointed to the first sentence of verse 3 and asked, "Brian, why does God want you to take a few minutes before offering this prayer to think about how richly He has blessed you?"

After a pause Brian answered, "I guess it will help me feel how much God loves me, and how much I love Him."

"That's exactly right," we agreed. "So please remember to do this." We then continued reading and paused again toward the end of verse 4, asking, "What does it mean to pray with *real intent?*"

Brian responded, "I suppose it means I need to be sincere about it."

"Not exactly," I said. "Sincerity is covered in the prior phrase. Praying with real intent means that you need to tell God what you intend to do if He answers your prayer." We discussed the implications that knowing the truth about these questions might have on the way Brian should conduct his life. We then read verse 5 and explained how God answers prayers, through thoughts that come into our minds and feelings in our hearts. I concluded, "Will you do this assignment, Brian?"

Brian said he would.

By the time Brian stood to leave, we had spent about 70 percent of our time in the living room understanding and answering Brian's questions, and 30 percent teaching him *how* to get his own answers in private, prayerful study of the Book of Mormon. The missionaries telephoned Brian on Saturday, asking if he had any questions about the homework assignment. Brian responded that he had blocked out two hours on Sunday evening to do it.

Following the opening prayer in our meeting with Brian on the following Tuesday, proudly and with a smile on his face, Brian handed typed copies of his homework to the elders and to us.

"Let me tell you what I learned," Brian began. He read his answer to the first question aloud. It began, "It makes God angry when people baptize infants because it trivializes the Atonement of Jesus Christ." He then explained how he had come to his conclusions. For ten minutes, he explained how he had distilled his answer from Moroni 8.

"Clay," Brian then said, "thank you for making me write it down. I *hate* to write, but writing it forced me to *think* about it. It really, really was helpful." Brian then went through the same process with his answers to the second and third questions, reading his answers aloud and then explaining how he had come to those conclusions from the two chapters. The answers were similarly insightful.

When Brian had finished reviewing his homework, he concluded, "And do you know what? I really believe that these things are true. I finally understand it in my head, and as I prayed I could feel in my heart that it is true." I noticed how carefully Brian handled the Book of Mormon in his hands as he said this. He clearly felt that he was holding something that was special.

I then asked, "Brian, now that you know this is true, will you be baptized?"

"I thought about it, and I really *want* to be baptized," Brian responded. "You told me that I needed to tell God what I intended to do, so I did. At first I thought I should wait until all my questions about the Mormon church have been answered. But then I realized that's not the purpose of baptism. If I wait until all my questions are answered, I'll be waiting forever. See, it says right here," he said, pointing at his answer to the second question, "the purpose of baptism is to make a commitment to God that we'll follow Him. Baptism is the start, not the finish." We agreed on a baptismal date of December 17.

Our friend, the investigator, had taken the first thirty-five minutes of the forty-five-minute lesson time to teach *us* the gospel and to bear *his* testimony to *us*. The missionaries could only briefly summarize the longer lesson they had prepared, but it didn't matter that there was little time. We all learn things more deeply when we teach them to others than when we listen, and Brian had spent thirty-five minutes teaching us the first principles and ordinances of the gospel.

The subsequent meetings with Brian went just as the first one had. Before we adjourned, I wrote down another homework assignment to help him find answers in the Book of Mormon to two of his other questions. When I began to write the seven steps on that sheet of paper, Brian said, "You don't need to write those again. I've got them down cold. Pray, read, write. Pray, read, write. Then pray again. It's a great system." Elder Adams reliably called between the meetings to be sure Brian understood and was doing his homework. Brian always took the first twenty minutes of the subsequent meetings to review what he had learned by doing his homework, and the missionaries taught for about fifteen minutes. We spent the last ten minutes explaining his next assignment and being sure Brian understood the other commitments that they were asking him to make. I baptized my friend Brian on December 17, 2005, in the Belmont chapel.

⌒

We learned several lessons from these extraordinary experiences with Brian that we've applied in each of the subsequent opportunities we've had with the missionaries to study the gospel with our acquaintances in our home.

First, as we first learned in our experiences with Stephen Spencer (mentioned in chapter 2), we have begun asking each person to come to these discussions with a list of questions about religion to which they've not been able to find satisfactory answers. The missionaries are taught in *Preach My Gospel* (pages 107–14) how *they* should study the Book of Mormon, to start with questions so that they can "liken all scriptures unto [themselves]" (1 Nephi 19:23–24). They are then taught to prayerfully search for answers in the scriptures, write down the thoughts and impressions that come to their minds as they study, and then pray to know if the things that they have concluded are true. If it is good for missionaries to study in this way, it is good for their investigators to do the same.

Second, in our prior experiences sharing the gospel with others, we had somehow just assumed that those we were teaching knew *how* to read the scriptures, just as we had assumed that Joshua Moore knew *how* to pray. So we and our missionaries had always spent a very large share of the time with our friends and investigators *teaching them.* We had behaved as if the *primary* occasion in which conversion occurs is when we are teaching the lessons to investigators. As a consequence, 90 percent of the time we spent in those discussions was consumed by the missionaries teaching and testifying. Meetings with the missionaries comprise a very important venue, of course. But we now see clearly that there is a second venue in which the converting power of the Spirit can come into the hearts of those who are investigating the gospel—that is, their privately and prayerfully studying the Book of Mormon to explore the answers God offers to the questions that they've been thinking about.

We and our missionaries now spend a significant portion of our time with investigators teaching them how to do this. And we spend a significant portion of our discussions with them asking *them* to teach and testify to *us* of the things they learned and felt while studying and praying. Christine and I are both teachers by profession, and we have taught innumerable classes in church. We know that we learn much more when we *teach* a lesson than when we *hear* a lesson. We now know that the same principle applies to those who are learning about the restored gospel. They learn it far more deeply when we give them the chance to teach us.

The third insight was spawned by Brian Carpenter's statement relative to his homework assignment: "I *hate* to write, but writing it forced me to *think* about it." This principle is right there at the bottom of Moroni 10:3: "Ye shall receive these things, and *ponder it in your hearts.*" I never had thought much about this element of the promise, and we never had taught our investigators how to ponder the truth in their hearts. It turns out that this is a *critical* element in the process of conversion.

I have spoken about "homework" with many members and missionaries. Often they counter with, "Brian had an MBA from Harvard. Homework comes easy to him. How about investigators who never finished high school? Are you assuming that they could answer those questions?" My answer is twofold. First, it is true that Brian isn't your typical investigator. But isn't it exciting that if we employ God's ways rather than man's, we actually can invite such people of capacity to learn of us, and that they can excitedly want to join our church? And second, not every person can answer these questions with the same articulate tongue as Brian. But that is the right answer to the wrong question. The right questions are these:

- Do we want to teach the gospel to people who have questions?
- Do we want them to think and ponder to know God's answers to their questions?

If so, homework that can be scaled to each person's background is a great tool.

And fourth, we have learned that a key reason why some of those we had invited to learn the gospel had declined our invitations, and why others had chosen to stop studying with our missionaries before baptism, was that we had been attempting to tell them what *we* thought *they* needed to know. If our answers didn't correspond with their questions, they judged the gospel to be irrelevant to their lives. By organizing each of our missionary lessons and the "homework" assignments we give them around questions that they've been trying to find answers to, many more of those we've invited have accepted our invitations.*

---

* *Preach My Gospel* states, "Adjust your teaching to meet needs" (177). It also tries to help missionaries (and all of us) learn to ask questions and listen so we accomplish exactly what is being said in this section (see 183–86).

CHAPTER 9

Teach How to Keep the Sabbath Day Holy

NOTES

Almost all of us have one or more "sacred places"—places where at earlier points in our lives we had warm, happy, memorable experiences. We love to go back to these places. I have several. One is the Jordan River in the Rose Park neighborhood of Salt Lake City. When I was thirteen, my brother Elliott, our friends, and I built kayaks, and we spent our teenage summers plying up and down the Jordan River. I love the Jordan River as it flows through Rose Park.

Another sacred place is the Queens College of Oxford University in England. Against all odds, I received a Rhodes Scholarship, and it was there as a graduate student studying late at night on the third floor of Drawda Hall on High Street that I learned for certain that Jesus Christ lives, that the Book of Mormon is true, and that His gospel actually has been restored to the earth.

Whenever time allows on my trips to Salt Lake, I walk along the Jordan River, and memories flow by, washing clear my concerns. Though I return to England less often, always I try to return to Oxford, where I sit on a bench on the other side of High Street to remember the Spirit that came into that room and changed my heart forever. I always leave Oxford with my spirit cleansed.

This description of sacred places, I hope, will put my comments in this chapter in context. In the two chapters above I asserted that the reason why many investigators don't follow through with their commitments to read, ponder, and pray is that we haven't taught them how to do these things. I pose a similar concern in this chapter: When people don't follow through with their commitments to attend church, it often is because they have never been to a Mormon worship service before, and they actually don't know how to do it. And if they come, the meetings often inadvertently "happen" to them, as if there isn't anything we or they can do about it. I'd like to suggest three things we might do differently.*

First, we can schedule meetings with our investigators in a church building before they come to Sunday services. Give them a tour of the building and tell them what goes on in every place: sacrament meeting, Relief Society, priesthood meeting, Primary, and so on. They need to know that the church building itself won't be intimidating. In fact, we want them to feel that the church building is a *sacred* place because people like to return to places that they consider sacred, places where they know they will feel good. This means that when we meet with them in the chapel, the missionaries need to teach them a *wonderful* lesson. We need to help them have a *great* experience *with* the Spirit *in* the building.

Although there are a lot of elements in conversion that are beyond our control, having a wonderful experience at church is not one of them. To illustrate that we can predictably have great

---

*These and other ideas to respond to the specific needs of the investigator (see *Preach My Gospel,* 148) can be discussed and planned, using the "Progress Record," as part of missionary coordination in Priesthood Executive Committee, ward council, and other planning meetings (see *Preach My Gospel,* 219).

experiences in church, I have pasted below an email that I sent to about ten of my friends in our ward a few months ago.

Dear friends:

As you may know, our missionaries, Christine, and I have been studying the gospel with Bill Skelley. He is making extraordinary process. Bill was the chairman of the Board of Selectmen in Belmont when we were working to get the permits required to build the temple, and Bill was very helpful in making sure that the hearings were fair. Bill has agreed to come to our fast and testimony meeting this Sunday. I am not in a position to tell you what to do. But if you feel inspired to do so, please include Bill in your fast this Sunday. And if you feel so inclined in the meeting, I'd be grateful if you could offer your testimony so that Bill can feel the truthfulness of what you will say. I am hoping that this meeting of the Belmont II Ward this Sunday will be the best fast and testimony meeting that has ever occurred since the church was organized in 1830.

With my deepest thanks in advance,

Clay Christensen

My friends truly fasted, prayed, and testified for Bill Skelley. I simply can say that I feel sorry for all the other members of the Church who could not attend this particular fast and testimony meeting in April 2012 in the Belmont II Ward. I can't imagine there has ever been a better one.

Every ward in the Church can bring the Spirit into their meetings. But it helps if they know which investigators are coming and what each person needs.

Second, think about how many times an investigator comes

to church for the first time late, wearing jeans and a T-shirt. He sits on the back row where families with noisy children sit. He looks at everyone else wearing their Sunday best, with friends and family, and thinks, "I don't fit here." Maybe the mistake we've been making is that we invite people to attend church without teaching them *how* to worship with us—how to get there, what to wear, where to sit, and how to benefit from what occurs.

Third, there are two commandments at issue here: The first is to partake of the sacrament on Sunday. The second is to keep the whole day a holy day. If an investigator attends church, many of us are prone to spike the football, declare victory, and walk off the field, only to realize later that we haven't crossed the real goal line, which is to keep the Sabbath day holy. Even when investigators feel the Spirit at church, that feeling can quickly dissipate when they fill the rest of the day with unholy activities.

We need to teach them how to honor the Sabbath day. We can do this by saying things like, "When you wake up on Sunday morning, kneel alone and with your family and pray. Tell Heavenly Father that you're going to church today. Ask for His help so that you'll be able to feel His spirit as you listen to the speakers and the teachers."

When we teach people about the Sabbath, we should not inadvertently teach that going to church is all that is required. I sometimes teach them by reading together Mosiah 13:16–19 and then asking questions such as, "What are some of the *unholy* things that people do on the Sabbath day?" It is easy to write down a long list. I then ask, "What are some of the *holy* things you could do on Sunday?" This is harder, but they need to write those down, too. Then I invite them, "Will you promise me that this Sunday you won't do *any* of these unholy things, and instead you'll fill your day doing these holy things?"

CHAPTER 10

Teach about Temptation: Our Opponents Are Not Passive

Satan is an able foe. When the kingdom of God is poised to move forward in a significant way, Satan never snaps his fingers and declares, "Troops, we've lost this one. Let's retreat and see if there is something easier for us to conquer." Rather, Satan always intervenes, often personally, to stop it.

For example, after God called Moses to lead Israel out of Egypt, Satan appeared to Moses, ranting and demanding that Moses worship him (see Moses 1:12–22). When Moses refused, he saw the bitterness of hell. As Jesus prepared for His ministry, He went into the wilderness to fast and pray. Satan knew what that implied, and he offered Christ the entire world if He would but worship him (see Matthew 4:1–11). And when the boy Joseph knelt to pray in the Sacred Grove, Satan knew that it signaled the Restoration of the gospel, and he intervened to try to stop it (see Joseph Smith–History 1:15–17).

In the same way, when our friends are preparing for baptism we should expect temptation and deception to intensify. This means, consequently, that our job as missionaries is to teach our friends how to identify temptation and withstand it. The onslaught comes in two forms. The first is personal temptation to disobey God's commandments. The second is apostasy.

Satan frequently captures new converts in a paradox on obedience. We teach our friends that if they give in to temptation, they should not quit trying to overcome it, because the Lord has offered repentance and forgiveness. Satan then uses this for his advantage, however, by teaching new converts, "Repentance is like a 'Get out of jail free' card. It's perfectly fine to give in occasionally and enjoy some of your old sins—when you're done you just repent, promise you won't do it again, and you are forgiven."

In my experience, a better way to arm new converts against the wiles of Satan is to teach that it is easier to keep the commandments 100 percent of the time than 98 percent of the time.*

The other way that Satan arrests new converts' progress is apostasy. This can happen before or after baptism, when someone is convinced that the Church isn't true after all. I have decided to offer a few of my thoughts about how this happens—because understanding Satan's deception that leads to apostasy is very much an element of missionary work.

Deception often comes from friends or relatives who honestly believe that they are saving our converts from sin. They seek to discredit the story of Joseph Smith or the Church and its current leaders. They often claim that certain doctrines and policies of the Church are false or out of date. As he has done from the beginning of time, Satan intervenes to attempt to stop new converts from being baptized. Or, if they have already been baptized, he will try to reverse what has been accomplished.

---

*See, for example, Thomas S. Monson, "The Three Rs of Choice," *Ensign*, November 2010, 67–70.

My approach here is to frame a way that Satan sometimes crawls into our minds and rewires our logic circuitry, causing us inadvertently to reach perverse conclusions from true data.

If you can, please put this book down for a minute and read again chapters 2 and 3 of Ether in the Book of Mormon. This section describes the brother of Jared, to whom I will refer as the Prophet. He had often talked with God, who spoke with him from within a cloud. The Prophet knew God. He had been chastened by God, and he knew how important it is to God that we pray often to Him.

The Prophet formed sixteen white stones and asked God to touch each stone with His finger. The Prophet was so surprised when he actually saw the finger of God touching the stones that he "fell down before the Lord, for he was struck with fear" (Ether 3:6). The Prophet then explained his reaction by saying, "I knew not that the Lord had flesh and blood" (v. 8).

The Lord then asked the Prophet whether he had seen more than just His finger. When he said no, the Lord offered to allow the Prophet to see Him in whole. God then introduced Himself to the Prophet by saying (in my language): "I'm actually not God. I am Jesus Christ, the Son of God—but it is okay for you to call me God. God and I are of the same heart and mind. I have been prepared from the beginning of the world to redeem mankind." God then explained to the Prophet that at that point He had a body that looked like ours, but it was the body of His spirit. He explained that in the future He would come to earth and live in a physical body like ours. Furthermore, God told the Prophet that this was the first time, from the creation of the world until that point, that anybody had been allowed to see Him.

By asking questions, the Prophet learned some fundamental dimensions about who God is that he simply had not previously understood. The Prophet's early concepts weren't wrong per se. But they were incomplete. The brother of Jared had to revise and to state differently his early concepts of God. The revelation about God was not a discrete event, in which all that could be known about God was delivered in a batch to His Prophet. It was a process over time. And I presume that at the end of this experience the brother of Jared had, there remained a lot about God that the Prophet still didn't understand.

Now imagine, after the Prophet had had these experiences and had begun teaching to others what he had just learned, that someone showed you two "snapshots" about the ministry of the brother of Jared. One snapshot had been taken early in the Prophet's journey, and the other snapshot had been captured toward the end. Your friend says to you, "Look at the inconsistencies between his first description of God versus the one that was written several years after the first one. Can you see how much he embellished the story? The guy is just a charlatan—and he's not a good charlatan, to boot, because he can't even remember what the story line was the last time he told it!"

What's going on here? The problem, at its core, is a wrong conception of revelation. By way of metaphor: Over the last thirty years the ways in which we teach biochemistry and molecular biology have changed dramatically. In reality, the laws of science in these fields have not changed at all. It is our understanding of these fields and therefore what we can teach that have changed. In the same way, God did not change. He is the same yesterday, today, and forever. It was what the Prophet knew about God, and what he could teach about God, that changed.

Some people criticize Joseph Smith because he embellished or revised things that he previously had said or written. They often conclude that because of these contradictions he must not have been a prophet. They have it exactly wrong. The fact that Joseph Smith actually changed something that he previously had said or written should not bother us. He in fact *was doing what prophets should do:* asking questions that previously had not been asked so that he could receive, and then convey to us, more of what God wanted us to learn.

Revelation is a lot like a detective movie. The protagonist (the Prophet) starts out with limited understanding of a complicated problem. As he asks question after question, the truth becomes clearer, but not without dead ends and wrong hypotheses based on limited information along the way. These movies end with the message on the screen, *To be continued . . .* (as in, " . . . we believe that He will yet reveal many great and important things pertaining to the Kingdom of God," stated in our ninth Article of Faith). There are many of these "movies" of the process of revelation. The "stars" of these other movies include Moses, Peter, Thomas, Joseph Smith, and others—prophets whose understanding of God came from iterating processes of questions, answers, and teaching; questions, answers, and teaching.

Perspective matters a lot. From God's perspective, the doctrine of Christ is complete and unchangeable. Some current or former members of our church pray that our prophets will change our doctrines or policies to conform to emerging societal norms. God does not invent the rules and doctrines on the fly to keep pace with society, however. From God's perspective, doctrine is unchangeable. But from *our* perspective, we must always expect that the doctrine that we understand *will always evolve and improve.* We should expect that the Prophet might change things, on occasion. But we must also believe that we, as members, might be wrong too—and we might need to be willing to change our position on a policy or belief as we learn more about the gospel of Jesus Christ.

We simply must pray that we might ask the right questions, questions that will lead to our knowing more of what God knows.

We desperately need to teach the members of our church the centrality of questions that lead to revelation. Converts rarely sneak into the Church without Satan noticing it. If we don't teach these things clearly, then the elect—really smart people—can get very confused, very quickly, before and after baptism (see Matthew 24:24).

Like every thoughtful convert, I still have a lot of unanswered questions. But I have no doubts that the gospel of Jesus Christ has been restored to the earth. We cannot be inoculated against apostasy. Satan has arrayed a set of sophisticated tools to attack the faith of friends who are naive about how revelation works. Teaching our members and our new converts about how revelation works, and how deception can be laid bare, are important elements of missionary work in our day.

> We invite you to visit frequently our website
>
> **everydaymissionaries.org**
>
> as you read this book. Tell other readers what you learn as you follow the principles for sharing the gospel—and tell your stories that will inspire the rest of us!

In this part we have discussed how we can help those who are investigating the gospel to resolutely work toward baptism. We need to teach our investigators that as members of The Church of Jesus Christ of Latter-day Saints, we are in essence attempting to learn, in incremental steps, what God knows. We need to teach them why the conversion process begins by asking questions the answers to which they previously had not been able to find, how to pray as if they are having personal discussions with God, how to find answers to their questions in the scriptures, and how to ponder what they are reading. We need to teach them how to renew their spirituality every week as they keep the Sabbath day holy, how the adversary works to destroy our faith, and how to stay faithful.

PART 3

BUILDING THE KINGDOM OF GOD

~

The kingdom of God typically is built one convert at a time. Because their experiences of conversion often were not recorded or published, the personal miracles by which some people joined the Restored Church are little known even to their progeny. I have opened my journal in the preceding chapters, hoping that you will conclude that you too can repeatedly witness the conversion of wonderful people because you have taught them how to become converted. I hope that you now can say, "I can do it. I now know how it happens."

Other stories about missionary work, however, are about large groups of people joining the Church, similar to the experience of Alma, who worked such miracles in the waters of Mormon. For example, Wilford Woodruff orchestrated the westward migration of nearly the entire population of the Fox Islands off the Maine coast. In England he brought hundreds of John Benbow's friends of the United Brethren into the Church. In our day, the pioneers in Ghana brought thousands into the Church, even before it was officially established there. In these accounts, however, the record essentially shows us what happened but offers less insight about how they did the work.

The purpose of the chapters in part 3 is to share some extraordinary miracles that happened in our day—to help you see how normal members of the Church, people like you and me, have introduced others to the Savior and His gospel and have seen and participated in miracles in building the kingdom of God. I personally saw these miracles occur or was able to interview people who were at the center of them. These miracles occurred, I believe, because they followed the thoughts and ways of God.

At the end of this section I will try to synthesize important principles from these events in a way to help bishops, ward mission leaders, families, and individual members realize that miracles like these can occur in your wards and branches too.

CHAPTER 11

Involving Everyone in Augusta, Maine

In September 2002, I was assigned to assist Elder Glenn L. Pace of the North America Northeast Area presidency in reorganizing the presidency of the Augusta Maine Stake. As we sought to learn whom the Lord would have us call as the new stake president, we asked the men we interviewed how they had come to belong to the Church. A startling number gave the same answer: "My parents were baptized into the Farmingdale Branch in 1963 when I was a boy." After hearing this several times, we inquired what had happened and were told that more than 450 people had joined the Church in that branch that year.

Before the general session of stake conference the next day, I was introduced to an elderly man and his wife in the audience, George and Karline McLaughlin. George had been president of the Farmingdale Branch at that time, and I subsequently returned to interview the McLaughlins in their home about their experience in leading the branch. On my return, I found George in failing health, confined now to his bed in the attic bedroom of their humble home where they had raised eight children in Gardiner,

121

Maine. As I listened to their memories, it became clear to me that I was in the presence of two of the humblest but mightiest missionaries in the history of the Church, and that their story needed to be told.

Brother and Sister McLaughlin joined the Church in 1951 due to a remarkable vision that Karline's mother had had. Their marriage was sealed in 1955 in the Logan Temple. At the time, there were five branches of the Church in Maine. The McLaughlins attended a branch of ten active members in Litchfield, near Augusta. The branch had grown to more than twenty active members by the early 1960s when George was called as branch president, and in 1962 the branch moved to a small building they had built in Farmingdale, another suburb of Augusta. Shortly after the move, George, who drove a milk delivery truck by profession, decided to fast and pray for two days in order to learn from the Lord how he should go about building the Church in the vast area of central Maine that comprised the Farmingdale Branch. On the second day, George pulled his milk truck to the side of a country road and found a secluded spot where he poured out to the Lord his desire to build the kingdom. As he returned to his truck, he came to understand through the Spirit what he and the members of his branch needed to do.

The following Sunday in a sacrament meeting address, George described his plan to the branch members—a talk that Sister McLaughlin recalled as one of the most inspiring and Spirit-filled she has ever heard. Following the meeting, President McLaughlin called three of the families in the branch to serve as "proselyting families." Each family had the assignment to bring another family to the church on the Wednesday evening ten days hence. At that meeting, which George called "U-Night," he would show a movie about the Church and then give a brief talk that concluded with his testimony. This was to be followed by the missionaries teaching a discussion to the family in their home later that week, and then by the missionaries teaching the next discussion to them at the church building during the next Wednesday's U-Night. They were to continue meeting with these families twice each week, once at the church and once in their homes, until the families were baptized or decided not to continue their investigation, at which point the proselyting families would need to find another family to bring to the next U-Night.

When the time of the first U-Night arrived, each of the proselyting families arrived with a family. In the interview I expressed surprise that these families had so faithfully accepted and delivered on this intimidating assignment from their branch president. Karline explained, "It was because of the talk George gave in sacrament meeting." Remarkably, each of the families they brought to the U-Night was baptized, and on the next Sunday George called each of these new families to serve as proselyting families as well.

When he met Brother and Sister McLaughlin shortly after arriving in 1963 to preside over the New England Mission, President Truman G. Madsen told George that if they ever baptized someone in the Farmingdale Branch, he would like to attend the service. A few weeks after the U-Night process had started, George invited President Madsen to a baptismal service but was told that his schedule would not permit it. When George reminded President Madsen of his promise, he countered, "How many are being baptized?" as if to test whether it was worth the three-hour drive from Boston. "I'm not going to tell you. Just come," was George's reply.

When President Madsen walked into the back of the Farmingdale chapel, he counted eighteen people sitting in white clothes waiting to be baptized. Tears came to his eyes. "George, I'll never see anything like this again in my life," he said in a hushed voice. "Yes, you will," was George's reply.

As more and more people were baptized and called to serve as proselyting families, the branch members had to alter their U-Night format. While the introductory film was being shown in the chapel, each of the missionary discussions was taught in a different classroom in the building so that if a family had studied the second discussion the prior week in their home, on Wednesday night they went to the room where the third discussion was being taught at the church. That year 451 people were baptized into the Farmingdale Branch; the next year, 191 people joined. They had to divide the branch over and over, of course. In each of the new units, they continued following the U-Night system.

"With so many people coming into what had been such a tiny branch, how did you keep them in the Church?" I asked.

"We had to teach them how to be Mormons," was Karline's reply. "You need to understand who these people were," she continued. "Most of them were poor and had little schooling." She and George reminisced about one family that literally lived in a log cabin with rags stuffed in the cracks to keep the wind out. "They stayed faithful, and eventually all four of their children graduated from college."

"My job as branch president was to teach them how to give talks and teach lessons in church. I had to teach them how to teach the gospel to their children. My counselors ran the branch. I trained the new members to become strong members," George added.

In the framework of retention that President Gordon B. Hinckley subsequently taught, these hundreds of new members had friends. They were brought to the Church by friends, and then they brought friends. They had responsibility. The Sunday after they were baptized they were called as proselyting families—a simple, clear call to bring another family, and then another, to the next U-Night. And they were nourished in the good word of God as they continued to learn and help teach these concepts again and again while helping their friends study the gospel with the missionaries.

Five years later, in 1968, Elder Harold B. Lee of the Quorum of the Twelve organized the Augusta Maine Stake. Ten of the twelve members of that original high council had been baptized into the Farmingdale Branch in 1963–64.

George McLaughlin, whose vision and faith had launched the Church in Maine on this trajectory, was not called to be the stake president or one of his counselors. "Someone came up to us in the congregation and asked if we felt badly not to have been called to lead the stake," Karline recalled. George broke in, "I told her that I was quite happy to sit with the people we loved and let others take the lead. That's why we did it, to bring others to Christ, not to bring any honor to us."

The contributions of many of the great missionaries in the early days of the restored Church have been broadly published. I was struck that in contrast, two of the greatest missionaries of this dispensation were living the final portion of their noble lives unheralded, in that small home in Gardiner, Maine. As we finished our conversation, however, I could sense that the deep spirit of peace in that room came from angels who were there patiently waiting so that, whenever their times might come, they could escort George and Karline McLaughlin, milk truck driver and mother, respectively, to heroes' welcomes in heaven.

CHAPTER 12

Visiting Those Who Did Not Come into the Fold

The stories in this and the next chapter show how leaders of a ward and stake can inspire members to bring converts into full fellowship in the Church. You will notice that I do not distinguish between less-active members and nonmembers because they both need conversion.

One of the most important skills that a leader needs to master is to ask the right question, because asking the right question is critical to knowing the thoughts and the ways of God. One example where we might be asking the wrong question, and consequently missing the thoughts and the ways of God, occurs every Sunday in every ward and branch in the church, when the question is asked: "How many people attended sacrament meeting today?" Our clerks walk up and down the aisles to count that number, and then they store that number in their offices for safekeeping so that they can fill out the quarterly report accurately.

Attendance numbers are important, but I can't help wondering if we are sometimes collecting the right answer to the wrong question as it relates to building the kingdom of God. The right question was framed by the Savior in His parable of the good shepherd: "How think ye? If a man have an hundred sheep, and one of them be gone astray, doth he not leave the ninety and nine, and goeth into the mountains, and seeketh that which is gone astray?" (Matthew 18:12). In other words, the Savior suggested that the right question is, "Who *didn't* come today?"

In the early 1990s, the Cambridge Ward that met in the Harvard Square chapel had more than 450 members, but well over half of them were inactive. Most of the inactive members lived in the communities of Malden, Everett, Revere, and Chelsea—working-class communities where it was quite easy to baptize people because they lived in circumstances that compelled them to be humble. But when these good people would brave their way to the Harvard Square chapel, they found a ward whose leadership ranks—in fact, all the ranks—were filled to overflowing with talented, experienced, qualified, lifelong members who had come to Boston to study at one of the great universities in the area. The vast majority of new members from these communities quickly felt that they didn't fit, and they fell into inactivity.

Facing this challenge, in 1990 our leaders decided to establish a "twig" (too small to be a branch) of the church in Malden. They held their first meeting in the home of Sister Letha May, who rarely had come to church but nonetheless had good feelings about it. Twelve people came on that first Sunday. Excited that they had attracted such a large group, they reported this to the stake president. In response, he told the members of the twig that if they got twenty people attending, he would rent a meeting hall for them to use on Sunday. So after the second sacrament meeting, those twelve members and two missionaries huddled together and asked themselves the question that the Savior said good shepherds ask: "Who is lost? Who else could have come here today but didn't?" They then each took an assignment to contact one of those people that same day, with the message, "We're starting a branch in our town. We missed you! Are you okay? Is there anything we can do to help? Can you come next week? We need you!" The next Sunday they set up twenty chairs in Sister May's living room, and after the meeting they again huddled to ask that same question, and answered it by taking assignments to contact those missing people that day.

Within a couple of months they had filled all twenty chairs. The stake president helped them rent a hall for their Sunday meetings and formally organized the "twig" as the Malden Branch. But they soon learned how inconvenient this was—they had to bring the podium, hymn books, sacrament equipment, and keyboard with them every Sunday and then take those things home again. They asked the stake president if they could rent the hall for the entire week. He said they could—as soon as they had forty members attending sacrament meeting. So the next Sunday they set up forty chairs to help them focus on who had not come: "Who else could have come today but didn't?" And "Who is going to contact them today to tell them how much we need them?" Within a year, forty people were attending, and they were able to lease the space week-round.

The members of the Malden Branch were feeling momentum, and they asked the stake president if he thought they might ever be able to have their own chapel. He responded that they could, but they needed to have attendance up to eighty people to qualify for a Phase I building. So the next Sunday they set up sixty chairs, and they kept having that meeting after church where they kept asking the right question. Within two years they had filled those chairs. The next Sunday they set up eighty and kept asking the question that is front and center in the mind of the good shepherd: "Who should have been here who didn't come today?" When they achieved their goal of eighty, the members decided it wasn't enough: They needed a second-stage building, which they could merit when 120 members were attending church.

When members of the Malden twig and branch were searching in their minds to answer the question, "Who didn't come?" the names that most readily came to mind were the less-active or occasionally active. Some of these less-active members readily began attending regularly when it became convenient. But many more of them responded when the invitation was, "The Church needs you." As the branch grew, the discussion in the "Who didn't come?" meetings focused increasingly on which of the missionaries' investigators could have been there but didn't come. Ultimately, as they kept trying to grow the branch, the question became, "Which of *my* friends didn't come because I didn't invite them?" In other words, "reactivation" was no longer the focus. Rather, they simply wanted to help those who should have been there but didn't come to join with them.

If work or vacation ever brings you to Boston, let me suggest that you visit one of the most beautiful buildings here. Drive north from downtown on Route 1, over the Tobin Bridge, and keep going for about seven minutes toward Revere. Just as you pass the Sargent Street exit, look to the left, where you'll see a beautiful second-phase chapel for the Revere I and Revere II wards, a monument to that small band of members who asked the question that good shepherds ask.

I've always wondered why the Savior preceded the telling of His parable of the good shepherd with the question, "What think ye?" Now I think I know. Perhaps, in our parlance, this would be phrased as, "What in the world are you *thinking* when all you do is count the number of my sheep that came into the fold every Sunday and then go home? The ones that *I'm* most worried about are those that didn't come!"

CHAPTER 13

Guiding the Weak
and the Simple: Twenty-Six
Branches in Queens

NOTES

In 1991, in the Queens Borough of New York City and the adjacent westmost portions of Nassau County on Long Island, there were two wards and two branches. These were comprised of about 250 active members of the Church and more than 1,000 inactive members of the Church. The Church was growing slowly. Although it was relatively easy to baptize new members in Queens, it was hard to keep them active, as the meetinghouses were hard to get to from many neighborhoods in Queens.

After many months of prayer and study, several Church leaders in New York City and Long Island decided to carve out Queens and the western portions of Nassau County from the New York City and Plainview (Long Island) Stakes in 1991 and give them to the full-time mission president (at the time this was Cree-L Kofford) as a mission district. This gave them more flexibility. These leaders divided the two wards and two branches into eight branches, each of which had about 30 active members and 150 to 200 inactive members. As needed, they rented street-facing facilities for the branches to meet in. This move plunged these branches into such a crisis of leadership that they each had to reach out to the periphery of the Church and draft members there into service as leaders, whether or not they were active or were keeping all of the commandments.

Within two years, sacrament meeting attendance in these branches had grown enough that they were divided in half again. Just as the branch leaders were feeling like they could operate their branches in an orderly way, they were forced by the divisions again to scour the fringes of the Church to find people whom they could recruit as leaders. As attendance at sacrament meeting again approached comfortable levels, the leaders divided the branches again, and so on. By 1999 there were 2100 members attending sacrament meeting in twenty-six branches in three mission districts in Queens and western Nassau.

There were many marvelous members and leaders who were the fruits of the prophecy made by Joseph Smith that the kingdom of God would be built by the weak and the simple (see D&C 1:18 23). Six of the leaders, with their spouses and children, however, stand out in my mind as having pivotal roles. They did not allow the not-as-yet leaders who were emerging from among the simple and weak to flounder and struggle to find their way. Rather, they were guided by this scriptural injunction: "And if any man among you be strong in the Spirit, let him take with him him that is weak, that he may be edified in all meekness, that he may become strong also" (D&C 84:106).

The first was Blair Garff, a district president twice and counselor to several mission presidents, who was responsible for training the leaders of all these branches and districts. He was an investment banker by profession, but on his weekends, year after year, he drove from his home in Westchester and combed the length and breadth of Queens, teaching and training the leaders of these emerging Church units. And when he had completed their training, he would look behind them to see a new cadre of leaders who had been newly called to serve, needing to be trained. While he did this, Susanne Garff took over much of what needed to be done at home. Blair and Susanne Garff were subsequently called to preside over one of the missions in Nigeria, and then to serve as temple president and matron in the New York Temple.

Ralph Weidler and Robert DeRosa were counselors to several mission presidents. While the presidents guided the full-time missionaries in the New York South Mission, Ralph and Bob drove fifty to sixty miles from Eastern Long Island several times each week to teach, guide, and interview members of the branches so that they could go to the temple in Washington, D.C.

David L. Duffy, M.D., joined the Church in 1973 after graduating from the Harvard Medical School. Like the Garffs, David and his wife, Audrey, trained hundreds of leaders in Queens during the decade as he served as president of the Queens East and West Districts. When the Queens Stake was created in 2005, President Duffy was called to serve as its first president, where he and Audrey continue training members to be great leaders.

One story tells you everything you need to know about President Duffy. Shortly before the Queens Stake was organized, I was assigned to visit the Queens West District conference as an Area Seventy. A few minutes before the general session was to begin, a man in his early twenties, quite upset, approached President Duffy. "President, you asked me to organize a Young Single Adult choir to perform today. I forgot."

President Duffy apologized to me that there wasn't going to be a choir, explaining that the young man who was supposed to convene a choir had never done anything like that before. I responded, "President, don't apologize. This is magnificent." I later reflected that if you define a "strong church" as one whose wards are fully staffed and in which every member magnifies his or her calling, then Queens is weak. But if "strong" means that year after year more people are baptized, more and more become active again in the Church, year after year more members are attending sacrament meeting and more members are becoming better leaders and teachers and striving to go to the temple, then Queens is one of the strongest places in the Church.

Jeffery Olson and his wife, Julie, lived in a comfortable home on Long Island, where he served as president of the Plainview Stake—which at the beginning of this story accounted for the eastern half of Queens and all of Long Island. As the Church continued to grow in Queens and the western portion of Long Island, it became clear to the Olsons that the Church needed their leadership skills more there than in the Plainview Stake. So they sold their home and moved to the border of Queens and Long Island through a miraculous set of circumstances. That is where they continued to raise their nine children. President Olson was released as stake president and called as the Lynbrook District president—a position in which he served for almost twelve years. The Olson children were typically among the few members their age in their branch, and they served in many callings as they grew up. I interviewed their son Peter when he came to Harvard for school:

"Have you taught Primary?"

"Yes."

"Have you served as a branch missionary?"

"I have."

"Can you play the piano?"

"No, the violin."

All before the age of nineteen, before he served his mission.

Peter is not unusual. All nine of the Olson children are

confident, capable, and committed members of the Church. After training hundreds of leaders in their branches and their district, Jeffery Olson was called as an Area Seventy in 2010.

The last person I'll mention is Hyrum Smith—a direct descendant of Joseph F. Smith and his father, Hyrum Smith, brother of Joseph the Prophet. Hyrum Smith lives in Queens. He served as one of the branch presidents for most of the time before, during, and after the events recounted here. Hyrum framed his calling as a trainer. When he called a new branch clerk, he dropped everything and spent two weeks training him so that the new clerk knew exactly what he needed to do, how to do it, when it needed to be done, and why. Then Hyrum would spend the next two weeks training his new elders quorum president in what, how, when, and why. And then he would drop everything and devote the next two weeks to teaching his new Relief Society president what, how, when, and why; and so on, and so on. And then he would realize that his branch had been divided and all of these capable, trained leaders were in the other branch or had moved away, and he had to train a whole new set of leaders. This happened again and again. Elder Olson told me that when he reads Doctrine and Covenants 84:106, he feels that it perfectly describes how Hyrum has worked to build his part of the kingdom of God.

I have come to frame these branches not as destinations but as bus stations. As new and newly active members follow the Lord's commandments and magnify their callings in the Church, they are magnified—not just as Saints of God but in their professions, too. These abilities become "tickets" that enable them to do more and better things in the Church as the branches grow and are divided. The tickets also enable them to move to new places to do new things. And for those who are leaders in the bus station such as those I've profiled above, they train, and train, and train—so that when their members get on another bus, they will be able to do what they will be asked to do. God's work is their work: "to bring to pass the immortality and eternal life of man" (Moses 1:39).

If business or vacation takes you to New York, take a couple of hours in Queens to admire some of the best architecture in the Church. Start by parking at any random point in Queens. Lock your car, and then just walk. You are within a twenty-minute walk of a beautiful LDS chapel. When you've admired it, walk another twenty minutes to the next chapel, and then twenty minutes to the next, and so on. You'll see a chapel in Rego Park that was designed and built by our church. The Woodside meetinghouse is a converted Bulova watch factory; in Flushing, the chapel was built by the Christian Scientist church nearly a century ago. In Richmond Hill it's a beautiful converted warehouse; and in Lynbrook, it used to be a business school. To me, these are beautiful, sacred places—not because of what they were but for what they are: testimonies to the faith of leaders and members whose thoughts and ways mirrored those of God.

CHAPTER 14

Building Wards That God Can Trust

NOTES

In my studies of how we can better build the kingdom of God, I have come to know three wards in which twenty to thirty new converts were routinely baptized, and most of their new members remained faithful. As best I can tell, there were not more "prepared" people living within the boundaries of these three wards than were living within the areas of neighboring wards. One ward is in a middle-class suburb of Dublin, Ireland; one is in a rural town in northern New England, where few are prosperous; and one is in a wealthy suburb of Boston.

Welcome to the Terenure Ward

A few years ago my family and I found ourselves over a weekend in Dublin, Ireland. We rented a car and drove south to a suburb, Terenure, to attend Sunday services in that ward. As I emerged from our car, about fifteen minutes before the services were to begin, I noticed a man on the other side of the parking lot. With a robust voice and hands raised high, he boomed out, "Could I be the first to welcome you to the Terenure Ward!" He then came over, introduced himself to us, helped us out of our car, escorted us into the chapel, suggesting where we might sit in order to best enjoy the meeting. In the process, he introduced me to more than twenty people.

In that sacrament meeting, three people who had been baptized the day before were confirmed members of the Church. And by chance, during the priesthood meeting that day the topic was missionary work. Someone asked the ward mission leader, who was leading this discussion, "How many new members have been baptized into the Terenure Ward this year to date?" (This was the end of May.)

"Counting the four people who will be baptized this week, twenty-three this year," the ward mission leader responded.

"Why is this happening to our ward?" the questioner continued. "We're in Ireland, in case nobody noticed. This is a Catholic nation. We're accustomed to baptizing one or two in a year. If we continue this pace, we might baptize fifty or so this year! Why is this happening?"

"You're right, in that in all the other wards in the stake they baptize one or two per year. I believe what has happened here, brethren, is that God trusts the Terenure Ward," the ward mission leader responded. "He trusts you because you invite people to learn about the gospel. He trusts you because you are always looking for someone who is new at church and making them feel loved and needed—before and after baptism."

The Lamoille Branch

When serving as an Area Seventy I sometimes had the chance to "tour" a mission and meet with the missionaries, and I always asked the missionaries in private conversations, "Is there a branch or ward in the mission where being assigned to work in that unit is viewed as if you have died and gone to heaven? And what is it about that unit that makes it so attractive an assignment for the missionaries?"

When I was meeting with missionaries in the New Hampshire Manchester Mission, *every* missionary I talked to wanted to be assigned to the Lamoille Branch, which is right in the northernmost portion of Vermont, bordering Quebec, Canada. In each of the prior three years, more than thirty people had been baptized into the branch.

"What is it about the Lamoille Branch that makes it so attractive to you?" I queried one of the elders.

He responded, "I don't know what it is. But if you can just get your investigators into the chapel up there, the members just wrap them into their arms and make them feel *so* welcome. It's funny. Even door-to-door finding works better in Lamoille than any other place in the mission." Tracting. Why did door-to-door finding work better in that place than any other in the mission?

Christine and I decided one free Sunday that we would drive from Boston to Lamoille Valley, about five hours northwest of Boston, to get a better sense of what made the branch work. I had learned from the stake president, Mike Sessions, that they had made the branch a ward a few weeks earlier. We interviewed many ward members and were repeatedly told how warm and welcoming the ward felt to new visitors. One recounted that the first time she attended church, a two-year-old girl came up to her with her arms outstretched—mimicking what she so often had seen adults do when someone new had walked through that door.

God seemed to trust the Lamoille Ward to love and care for his children.

The Weston Ward

At the time of this story, the Weston Ward encompassed several of the most affluent suburbs on the west side of Boston. Between 1967 and 1977, nearly three hundred people were baptized into the Weston Ward, about thirty converts each year. This included nineteen complete families. Most of these converts stayed active in the Church. In the process of interviewing for and writing a history of the Church in the Boston area, we spoke with many members and converts who lived in the ward during that period.

There is absolutely no pattern in how these people found the Church. Some were referred by members. Others were found by missionaries who knocked on their door. Quite a few found the Church on their own. But the one thing that they uniformly reported was that the minute they walked into the Weston Ward chapel, they felt loved. One of them said, "It was as if everybody was sitting backward in the pews to watch for me when I walked through the door."

For example, on one Sunday Sister Virginia Perry, whose husband, L. Tom Perry, was president of the Boston Stake, noticed a woman who had quietly found a space on the back row in the Weston chapel, having arrived a few minutes late for sacrament meeting. She was wearing jeans and a T-shirt and had come on her motorcycle. Sister Perry quickly sensed that the woman felt that she didn't fit in. Everyone else was wearing their Sunday best and was sitting with their families. So Sister Perry left her family alone, went to the back pew, and asked the visitor if she would mind if she sat beside her. When the woman smiled in the affirmative, Sister Perry put her arm around her. The next Sunday Sister Perry came to church wearing Levi's and a T-shirt.

The only explanation I have for why the Weston Ward baptized thirty people year after year, while the other wards in the area typically baptized only a few people each year, is that God trusted the Weston Ward. He knew that when His children prayed to Him for help and guidance, if He could just guide them to the Weston Ward or one of its members, He could trust the members to take it from there.

In all three cases I have described, the missionary work in the adjacent wards was tepid, but in these three wards it was brisk. I suspect that within the boundaries all of the branches and wards in the stakes where the Terenure, Lamoille, and Weston Wards were located, there were people who were praying to God in their own ways, asking for help about one thing or another. If God cannot trust the members of the Church to invite these people to learn His gospel, why would He put them in our path? And if God can't trust us to make His children feel loved and needed after they join the Church, why would God guide these people there in the first place?

I don't believe that more people were praying to God for guidance in these three wards' areas than in areas of other wards in their vicinity. The difference is that God trusted the members in these three wards; He answered the prayers of many of His children by putting them in the paths of the members or by guiding them to meet members at church.

Meriting the trust of God isn't new. Recall what he said about Abraham: "And the Lord said, Shall I hide from Abraham that thing which I do; seeing that Abraham shall surely become a great and mighty nation, and all the nations of the earth shall be blessed in him? *For I know him, that he will command his children and his household after him, and they shall keep the way of the Lord,* to do justice and judgment; that the Lord may bring upon Abraham that which he hath spoken of him" (Genesis 18:17–19; emphasis added).

I believe the same principle is at work at the level of the individual. In almost every ward, four to six people find 80 percent of the referrals that their wards submit for the missionaries to teach, year in and year out. Is it the case that these few good member missionaries have just been blessed to live around and work with all of the "golden" potential investigators? And is it plausible that the people who simply aren't engaged in missionary work have been cursed to live and work among those who have no interest in learning of the gospel?

I suspect that God might say about many "active" members of the Church today, "I know them, and I'm actually not sure whether they will do what I have commanded them to do in sharing my gospel with others of my children." God has promised that He will answer the prayers of His children. If He can't trust us, then He must use other means to answer the prayers of others.

CHAPTER 15

Jaime Valarezo and the Cambridge Spanish Branch

NOTES

Starting in 1976, a small group of Spanish-speaking members began meeting in their own Sunday School class in the Cambridge First Ward. By 1980 there were enough Spanish-speaking Saints that a dependent branch had been organized. Shortly after this a Spanish-speaking sister missionary, Carmen Francisco, was assigned to this branch. During her tenure in the branch she and her companions brought about fifty people into the Church. Most of these were sisters, many with young children, who were baptized without their husbands. After Sister Francisco was released from her mission, she reported home in California, but then returned to Boston and found employment. She was quickly called to serve as Relief Society president of the Cambridge Spanish Branch. At the time the branch had about forty active adult women and about six active adult men.

Sister Francisco challenged the Relief Society sisters to work on this issue, pointing out that if the branch were ever going to become a ward, they needed greater priesthood strength. The sisters determined to fast and pray over an entire weekend, asking

God to send through the doors of the Cambridge chapel on that Sunday a man who could become a great leader in the branch. So they fasted, and sure enough, that Sunday a new man walked through the door of the church building. But far from being the mature, capable leader they had fasted for, this young man was a fifteen-year-old immigrant from El Salvador, Jaime Valarezo, who had joined the Church there with his mother. Jaime stuttered so badly that he could not carry on a conversation with anyone except young children.

Sister Francisco muttered to her counselor as they left the meetings that day, "I can't believe that this is all that God sent us, after we fasted and prayed with such faith."

That wasn't the end of the story, however. Jaime had a big heart. He came early to church to put out the Spanish hymn books and prepare the sacrament. And it turned out that Jaime had a wonderful way with children. When children would fuss during meetings, he would pick them up and play with them. The children grew to love Jaime. One day the missionaries were teaching a couple in the church building, and they asked Jaime to look after their children so the parents wouldn't be distracted. The children enjoyed Jaime so much that they lobbied their parents to go back to church where Jaime was, and eventually the whole family was baptized. The missionaries began to take Jaime with them regularly whenever his care of children would help the parents focus better on what the missionaries were teaching. This combination worked, and the branch began to strengthen.

One day as sacrament meeting drew to a close the branch president called upon Jaime to offer the closing prayer. There was an audible gasp in the audience—people couldn't believe the branch president could be so insensitive to his speech handicap. But Jaime stood and offered a beautiful prayer. Members commented afterward that Jaime could now talk to children and to God—just not adults, yet. But that was to come. Jaime decided to fulfill a mission, and he was blessed by the stake president, Gordon Williams, that he would become fluent of tongue.

Jaime fulfilled a wonderful mission and gave a powerful, spirit-filled homecoming sacrament meeting talk to the (much larger) Cambridge Spanish Branch. It was stunning. In not many years, an insecure boy who couldn't speak to adults had become a man who stood before them confident, articulate, and filled with the Spirit of God. After the hymn and benediction at the end of Jaime's talk, no one rose to leave—they all just wanted to sit in the chapel and soak in the spirit that was in the room. Finally a teenage boy arose and spontaneously bore his testimony. "I just wanted to thank Jaime for all he has done for me," he said. "And I want Jaime to know that when I turn nineteen, I'm going to fulfill a mission just like he did." Then another boy arose, bore his testimony, thanked Jaime, and pledged that he too would fulfill a mission when he turned nineteen. One by one, thirteen of the boys in the congregation arose and made that pledge to Jaime.

Twelve of the thirteen boys fulfilled their pledges.

Today there are in the Boston area four Spanish-speaking units: two wards and two branches. The fasting and prayers of the Relief Society sisters of the Cambridge Spanish Branch were answered more powerfully than they ever could have hoped—but in God's ways.

CHAPTER 16

The Thoughts and the Ways of God

The howling winds from prosperity and secularism are working again against those who are trying to succeed in their missionary efforts in the prosperous and proud nations of the earth. Jeremiah saw what missionary work would be like in our day: "I will take you one of a city, and two of a family, and I will bring you to Zion" (Jeremiah 3:14).

Despite this diligent effort, however, Jeremiah saw that in our day most people will have little apparent interest in the gospel: "And it shall come to pass, when ye be multiplied and increased in the land, in those days, saith the Lord, they shall say no more, The ark of the covenant of the Lord: neither shall it come to mind: neither shall they remember it; neither shall they visit it; neither shall that be done any more" (Jeremiah 3:16).

Though this is the pattern that surrounds us, the stories recounted in this section occurred not in the days of Enoch, Ammon, or Wilford Woodruff, but in our day. My first instinct has been to refer to these as modern-day miracles. But is this true? It depends on your perspective: "For my thoughts are not your thoughts, neither are your ways my ways, saith the Lord. For as the heavens are higher than the earth, so are my ways higher than your ways, and my thoughts than your thoughts" (Isaiah 55:8–9).

I believe that the reason these remarkable people succeeded in the face of today's apparent indifference toward religion is that these member missionaries tried to know and follow God's thoughts and His ways as best they could. I believe that the miracles that occurred in their lives will be predictable in our lives too—when *we* follow His thoughts and ways as well. Let's examine these accounts through this lens.

The Simple and Weak

The leaders who initiated the growth in Queens had extraordinary personal capabilities. Rather than search for comparably capable leaders who could lead the Queens Ward, however, they put their faith in the Lord's promise that He would build the kingdom on the shoulders of the simple and weak:

"The weak things of the world shall come forth and break down the mighty and strong ones, that man should not counsel his fellow man, neither trust in the arm of flesh—but that every man might speak in the name of God the Lord, even the Savior of the world; that faith also might increase in the earth; that mine everlasting covenant might be established; that the fulness of my gospel might be proclaimed by the weak and the simple unto the ends of the world, and before kings and rulers. Behold, I am God and have spoken it" (D&C 1:19–24).

Rather than trying to rely on the leaders whose arms were strongest, they plunged themselves and the members into such straits that they *had* to rely on the simple and weak. They wanted *every* person in Queens to be able to speak in the name of God the

Lord, and believed that faith would increase in Queens if they allowed the weak and the simple to proclaim God's gospel.

Miraculously but predictably, the number of people attending sacrament services in Queens grew from 250 to 2100 in eight years.

When the Relief Society sisters in the Cambridge Spanish Branch fasted and prayed for a powerful priesthood leader, the Lord sent Jaime—and then magnified him. God answered the sisters' prayers beyond what they had imagined would be possible.

FRIENDS, RESPONSIBILITY, AND NOURISHMENT IN THE WORD OF GOD

George and Karline McLaughlin followed the counsel of President Gordon B. Hinckley, who reminded us, as did Moroni (see Moroni 6:4–5), that new converts need friends, responsibility, and nourishment in the good word of God. The McLaughlins followed this pattern assiduously. Everyone in the branch was brought by a friend, and then they brought friends. They were given responsibility the day after baptism to be proselyting missionaries. As these members recurrently helped the missionaries teach the gospel to their friends, they were repeatedly nourished in the good word of God. Predictably, not miraculously, hundreds of people accepted baptism, and most of these converts stayed committed to the faith.

THE GOOD SHEPHERD

The band of twelve members of the tiny Malden "twig" in the Boston Stake, anxious to have their own branch and chapel, followed the Savior's model of a good shepherd:

"How think ye? if a man have an hundred sheep, and one of

them be gone astray, doth he not leave the ninety and nine, and goeth into the mountains, and seeketh that which is gone astray?" (Matthew 18:12).

They gathered weekly after church to ask the Good Shepherd's question: "Who could have been here today that didn't come?" There are no mountains in Revere, Everett, Malden, and Chelsea, Massachusetts. But their serpentine byways were just as daunting to these members as the mountain was for the shepherd when he followed the paths on which his sheep had gone astray. When eight years later as members of the Revere II Ward they attended the dedication of their beautiful chapel, it was indeed a miracle. But it was predictable for them, as it will be for us.

Love One Another

Three wards—Terenure, Lamoille, and Weston—so earned the trust of God that they baptized dozens of people each year, even while the adjacent wards struggled to find a few new members. Reliably, when people came into the buildings of these three wards, they felt loved:

"By this shall all men know that ye are my disciples, if ye have love one to another" (John 13:35).

Is it remarkable that door-to-door finding went better in the Lamoille Valley than anywhere else in the mission? That in Terenure they could baptize twenty-three people in five months— in Ireland? I really think that during particular periods of years, God trusted members of these three wards. The remarkable number of people who joined the Church was indeed a miracle. But for the rest of us whose wards can become wards that God trusts, it is predictable.

My sense is that in each of these wards, the number of people joining the Church has regressed to the mean, suggesting that trust can be built but it can also wane.

Each of these members and leaders were entrepreneurs in Zion. They rightly assumed that the power was in *their* hands to bring to pass much righteousness. Here is their scriptural license:

"For behold, it is not meet that I should command in all things; for he that is compelled in all things, the same is a slothful and not a wise servant; wherefore he receiveth no reward. Verily I say, men should be anxiously engaged in a good cause, and do many things of their own free will, and bring to pass much righteousness; for the power is in them, wherein they are agents unto themselves. And inasmuch as men do good they shall in nowise lose their reward. But he that doeth not anything until he is commanded, and receiveth a commandment with doubtful heart, and keepeth it with slothfulness, the same is damned" (D&C 58:26–29).

A sense among some in the Church is that obedient Saints are those who follow the programs of the Church assiduously, and that innovation is a symptom of rebellion if it hasn't been "approved." These Saints followed the Spirit in an unscripted way. The programs of the Church are designed to leave room for a great deal of individual initiative and personal guidance. Indeed, an expiration date has not yet been appended to the last clause in the ninth Article of Faith (italics mine): "We believe all that God has revealed, all that He does now reveal, and *we believe that He will yet reveal many great and important things* pertaining to the Kingdom of God."

I believe that if we approach this work through the thoughts and ways of God, it is perfectly predictable that we will be instruments in bringing many more people to the Lord than historically has been the case. Indeed, this is what the Lord promised, and what He gave to His Saints described in the chapters that you have just read: "I will go before your face. I will be on your right hand and on your left, and my Spirit shall be in your hearts, and mine angels round about you, to bear you up" (D&C 84:88). "I will bear [you] up as on eagles' wings; and [you] shall beget glory and honor to [yourself] and unto [the Lord's] name" (D&C 124:18). The same promises are available to you and to me.

My Testimony

The choice to cobble together this book of stories from my own life and the lives of those I know well was a hard one because I have tried very hard to stay out of life's spotlight. But I adopted this approach because I wanted to describe not just *what* I've learned about sharing the gospel, but *how* I have learned, little by little, about the thoughts and ways of God.

The principles in this book have not emerged from a focused analysis of missionary work. The reason for this is that I think about missionary work every day. But I also think every day about how to be a better teacher at Harvard; how to be a better husband and father; how to build better companies; how to truly build the kingdom of God, just as Daniel foresaw. For whatever reason, I think and study about all of these (and many more) problems every day. In retrospect, I simply have been trying to learn fundamental truths and falsehoods that affect us.

In this pursuit, step by step I have concluded that many of the roadblocks that constrain missionary work are of our own making.

The growth of the Church in these last days is not dictated by the cycle of pride. What constrains the kingdom of God is that we tend to do our member missionary work according to the thoughts and methods of man. There is more that we need to learn about these issues. But I witness that the principles summarized in this book are true. I have learned them from the Spirit as I have tried to share the gospel.

Sharing the gospel will not compromise your success or your stature in your profession, your home, or your community. The Savior promised: "But seek ye first the kingdom of God, and his righteousness; and all these things shall be added unto you" (Matthew 6:33). In other words, the causal mechanism by which you will become successful in these other things is by seeking first the kingdom of God. These other things will not be added passively to you. The Spirit of God will magnify you so that you can do things that otherwise you would not be able to do. I know from personal experience that this is true.

I invite you to bring the promises that God has made in the Doctrine and Covenants, which are summarized in the introduction of this book, into your home and your heart starting today.

As your colleague in this work, I know that God lives and that Jesus Christ truly is the Savior of mankind. I know that they appeared to Joseph Smith, a boy. Through the power of God he translated the Book of Mormon. It is a true book. God and His Son have restored the true gospel to the earth in our day. I know these things of myself, directly from heaven.

I am grateful beyond words to have the truth, and to have the opportunity to link arms with you to share with all this magnificent gospel, with pride and with love.

—CLAYTON M. CHRISTENSEN
Missionary